Tale-Gating
with
Rebel Greats©

Best loved, first-hand football stories
from Ole Miss Rebel football greats,
plus their favorite tailgating recipes.

Compiled & Edited
by
Debra Dottley Brumitt

Designed
by
Woody Brumitt

Copyedited
by
Melissa Yow

Tale-Gating with **Rebel Greats**©

P.O. Box 820262
Vicksburg, MS 39182

Copyright © 1997
by
Tale-Gating with *Rebel Greats*

ISBN: 0-9658832-0-5

First Printing: July 1997

To order **Tale-Gating with Rebel Greats** please send $16.95 plus $3.50 shipping & handling per copy to P.O. Box 820262, Vicksburg, MS 39182. Mississippi residents add $1.19 per copy for sales tax.

Printed in the USA by

WIMMER

The Wimmer Companies, Inc.
Memphis

Dedication

This book is dedicated
to my father
John "Kayo" Dottley
who has always believed in and encouraged me.

He is, indeed, my hero.

and

To my mother
Nina Nosser Dottley
who has loved me unconditionally,
even when the conditions weren't perfect.

I love you both, too much.

Acknowledgments

We appreciate the help of these former Ole Miss football players. Without their support, **Tale-Gating with Rebel Greats**© would not have been possible.

Billy Ray Adams
Warner Alford
Billy Brewer
Johnny Brewer
Allen Brown
Perian Conerly*
Bobby Crespino
Doug Cunningham
Eagle Day
Kenny Dill
John Dottley
Doug Elmore
Ken Farragut

Mike Fitzsimmons
Charlie Flowers
John Fourcade
Bobby Franklin
Jake Gibbs
Larry Grantham
Glynn Griffing
Parker Hall
Harry Harrison
Stan Hindman
Junie Hovious
Robert Khayat
Jimmy Lear

Brian Lee
Kris Mangum
Archie Manning
Crawford Mims
Chris Mitchell
Barney Poole
Ray Poole
Richard Price
Todd Sandroni
Marvin Terrell
Wesley Walls
Ben Williams

Tale-Gating with Rebel Greats is a collection of stories and recipes from former Ole Miss football players who distinguished themselves during their tenure at Ole Miss. The stories are true, or so the authors say, but none of the recipes have been kitchen tested, so try at your own risk.

5% of the wholesale sales of **Tale-Gating with Rebel Greats** are donated to The J.W. Davidson All American Scholarship sponsored by the M Club Alumni Chapter of Ole Miss.

*On behalf of Charlie Conerly.

Table of Contents

*by Perian Conerly

Table of Contents

Table of Contents

Ole Miss Football...

Close your eyes and conjure up your best Saturday. The breeze in the Grove sends just enough cool air to tickle your toes. So many kids throwing so many footballs that when you look up, it's raining pigskins. Your taste buds set for another barbecue, chicken leg or sandwich prepared the night before with tender-loving care. And another drink of whatever you prefer in your red plastic cup.

And the talk, oh, the talk. Everywhere people talking Ole Miss football; anticipating the game at hand and reminiscing about past days of glory. Tales of Archie Who?, Billy Cannon's run, John Vaught, winning the SEC championship, who was an All American when, where they played pro ball and who the hottest recruits are for next season.

Then, before you know it, the band plays, and the Rebels are walking down the sidewalk, through the Grove, on their way to play their hearts out for the best fans in the world, Ole Miss fans.

I grew up on Ole Miss football. I think the first "poem" I ever learned was *Hotty Totty*. My mom, an Ole Miss cheerleader, and my dad, an Ole Miss All American, taught my brothers, sisters and me every cheer and song they ever knew, and we knew them too.

I have vivid memories of getting up before daybreak on Saturdays when Ole Miss played in Oxford. We'd load up in the station wagon and head from Vicksburg to Oxford, singing Ole Miss songs all the way. We'd pass carloads of other Ole Miss faithful, wave and honk, sharing excitement through closed car windows.

My favorite part of the day was eating in the Ole Miss cafeteria. That's where we tailgated. I still remember having the best pecan pie in the world there. It seems as if dad knew everyone, and that we stayed there forever, but eventually we headed to the stadium to watch the Rebels play. Our excitement grew every step of the way.

I thought we always won. We didn't. But when you're young, excited and it's a football day at Ole Miss, you just didn't lose.

Now I'm somewhat older, but when I go back to a football game at Ole Miss, I feel like a kid again. I love getting to the Grove early in the morning, setting up the food, and inviting old friends and new to join my family for our picnic. There's nothing so right in the world as being a part of the Ole Miss family and making the Ole Miss family a part of you. That's why we fans are so special.

So, it is with much excitement I bring you **Tale-Gating with Rebel Greats**©. Please enjoy the stories and favorite recipes of these outstanding Ole Miss football players. Share them with your friends, your children, and your family. After all, that's what we do best in the South–tell great stories and eat good food.

Go Rebels!

Debra Dottley Brumitt

Debra Dottley Brumitt
Editor

We wish to thank the following members of the Ole Miss family for their help in compiling *Tale-Gating with Rebel Greats*©

Langston Rogers
Assistant Athletic Director for Sports Information

Ed Meek
Assistant Vice Chancellor for Public Relations & Marketing

Roger K. Lyles
Director of Licensing

Robert Jordan
Cover Photographer

Chyna Ward
Secretary to Head Football Coach

Betty Drewrey
Athletic Department
Executive Secretary

Publications Department

10

Hotty Totty

Are You Ready?

Hell Yeah, Damn Right!

Hotty Totty

Gosh a' mighty

Who in the hell are we?

Hey

Flim, flam, bim, bam,

Ole Miss by Damn!

John Vaught

When I called to ask Coach John Vaught if I could come see him about a book I was writing, there was not a moment's hesitation before he said yes, come on, in fact you can come tomorrow. I was at his home the following day. I rang the doorbell and his wife, Eleanor, appeared with a big smile and a friendly welcome. I immediately felt right at home. The afternoon flew by, and before I knew it, it was over. I can't remember when I've been so awed by the presence of a man. I relish the memory of that Sunday afternoon.

John Vaught's tremendous coaching job at Ole Miss can be summed up by his 25-year record as head coach. He won 190 games, lost 61 and tied 12. What an incredible feat. He is known throughout the country as a football genius, but it takes more than genius to put together the kind of program he built at Ole Miss. It takes a man full of compassion, understanding and a genuine love of the sport and the men who play it, qualities John Vaught epitomizes.

Of his fondest memories, I thought he'd tell me about winning the games that escalated his career. He did. But he was really proud that most of his former players became fine, outstanding citizens. He felt honored that he might have had a little something to do with how they had developed.

"I tried to treat my players like a father would a son. When they needed guidance, I guided them, and when they needed discipline, I saw to it that they got it," he said.

I doubt you'd find many of his players who would disagree with that. Quite a tribute, don't you think?

Vaught now spends his time playing golf, hunting and taking care of his sprawling ranch just outside of Oxford. And, when asked, giving interviews.

**John Vaught
Rebel Head Coach
1947-1970 & 1973**

My First Walk

I still remember my excitement at being named head football coach at Ole Miss. Having an opportunity to coach at a university with a long and well respected football history, loyal fans, and a team eager for victory was a dream come true for me.

Right from the start, I knew Ole Miss was different from other schools where I had coached. As I traveled the state, I met hundreds of fans and alums, and they all made me feel a part of the Ole Miss family. They were inquisitive about the program we were going to build, what I thought about the upcoming season and how many games we were going to win.

Finally, our first home game arrived. It was September 9, 1995, and we were playing Indiana State. Keep in mind we had lost our season opener at Auburn, so I wasn't sure what kind of reception I'd get from the Ole Miss faithful.

I knew Coach Billy Brewer had started the tradition of walking the team through the Grove, and I had made up my mind we weren't going to change that. I had heard that both the fans and the team looked forward to this "March to the Stadium," and although I was looking forward to it, I really didn't know what to expect.

My son, Tucker, and I got to Kinard Hall and I summoned the troops. No sooner had we gotten down the hill, heading to the Grove, than the noise, cheering, clapping, back-slapping and hoopla began. People everywhere stopped what they were doing and cheered us on. By the time we had reached the Grove, a sea of fans–lined up on both sides of the walk and ten rows deep–was going wild. The crowd didn't thin until we got to Starnes Center.

I was overwhelmed. Here I was walking with my son, my football team and my staff to coach my first football game in Vaught-Hemingway Stadium, and the Ole Miss family was there with us. I looked around trying to take it all in, making a memory to last a lifetime. Out of the corner of my eye, I saw my mother, Olive, always my most faithful and loyal supporter, right out there in the crowd. I didn't know who was prouder, she or me, but I did know right then and there that Ole Miss was a place like no other.

Tommy Tuberville

Tommy Tuberville
Head Football Coach
Ole Miss Rebels

Billy Ray Adams

Position & Years　　　　　　**Nickname**
Fullback 1959-61　　　　　　　Tiger

All American 1961　　　　　　Miss. Sports Hall of Fame
All SEC 1961　　　　　　　　Ole Miss Sports Hall of Fame
Team of the Decade 1959

Organized Time

by Billy Ray Adams

While playing against Arkansas one year, one of our offensive linemen came back to the huddle and asked that we call a time-out to get organized because the Arkansas players lined up on him and he was getting killed.

Our exasperated quarterback said, "Hell, no, we're not going to call time-out to get organized because while we're getting organized, they'll be getting organized too. And if they get any more organized than they are right now, I don't want any part of them."

Ah...Sweet Revenge

by Billy Ray Adams

The greatest victory I can remember was beating LSU in the Sugar Bowl in 1960.

Not many of us will ever forget the shattering defeat they gave us during the regular season. Future Heisman Trophy winner and LSU Tiger Billy Cannon's famous punt return for a touchdown still reruns in my mind.

But not this night, not the Sugar Bowl; victory was going to be ours. Billy Cannon was held to a minus 8 yards rushing for the Sugar, and we beat them 21-0.

We won the National Championship after that Sugar Bowl. And who said revenge isn't sweet? I still like the taste of that win.

What Coach Vaught said:

Billy Cannon's run was an absolute fluke. Jake Gibbs, our punter, was good and accurate. It was pretty windy that day. In fact, we kicked on third down because of the wind situation and LSU's potential to block the kick. The ball hit about ten yards from where Billy Cannon was standing. It took a horizontal bounce right to him. He caught it on the dead run. He just took off down the sideline. Five or six of our guys missed him. He went right by me on the sideline. I thought about running out there to try and tackle him, but I was afraid I'd miss him too.

17

Corn Dip

1 c. shoe peg corn, drained
6 green onions, chopped
1 green pepper, chopped
1 jalapeño pepper, chopped
1 or 2 T. mayonnaise
4 tomatoes, seeded, chopped and drained on paper towel
seasoned salt and lemon pepper to taste

Mix and serve with corn chips or wheat crackers. Keep refrigerated until picnic time and be sure to store in your ice chest before you head to Vaught-Hemingway.

Apache Bread

1 loaf French bread
16 oz. sharp cheddar cheese
1 8 oz. carton sour cream
½ c. green onions, chopped

1 tsp. Worcestershire sauce
2 4 oz. cans green chiles
1 c. ham, chopped

Preheat oven to 350 degrees. Split loaf in half. Scoop out center of bread and press bottom loaf flat. Combine all other ingredients and fill bottom half of loaf. Cover with the top half, wrap in foil and bake 1 hour. Good served cold.

Billy Ray Adams
Madison, Mississippi

Billy Ray Adams was drafted by the San Francisco 49er's in 1962. Unfortunately, he was injured in an automobile accident two days after the Ole Miss-Mississippi State game, which prevented him from pursuing a professional football career.

The J.W. Davidson
All American Scholarship

The J.W. Davidson All American Scholarship, sponsored by the M Club Alumni Chapter of The University of Mississippi, is named in honor of Coach Wobble Davidson. Coach Davidson was a former long-time member of the Ole Miss football staff as well as student M Club advisor.

The M Club scholarship is an effort of former athletes to help their own. Dedicated to serving children of former M Club Members, each $4,000 scholarship is awarded yearly to at least two students. Selection is based on need and merit. Recipients must remain in good academic standing to keep the scholarship.

The M Club Alumni Chapter is made up of some 1,800 former varsity letter winners at The University of Mississippi. The primary function of the chapter is to keep the rich traditions of Ole Miss sports alive by supporting the University, the Athletic Department, coaches and student athletes.

The group sponsors several events throughout the year including reunions for various team sports. It also makes periodic donations of memorial books to the University Library in honor of its deceased members.

The Ole Miss Sports Hall of Fame is a project of, and sponsored by the M Club Alumni Chapter. Founded by the group in 1986, this Hall of Fame recognizes former Ole Miss standouts for their contributions to Ole Miss athletics.

Funds for these and other projects are raised throughout the year from members' contributions and private donations. The Red-Blue Game is the largest fund raiser for the scholarship endowment. In exchange for selling tickets, working the gates and performing other tasks, the Athletic Department makes a contribution to the scholarship endowment.

Mike Robbins, President
M Club Alumni Chapter

Warner Alford

Position & Years
Left Guard 1958-60

Nickname
Boon

Team Co-Captain 1960
Distinguished American Award

Team of the Decade 1959

Memories

by **Warner Alford**

I was fortunate to be a student athlete at Ole Miss and then come back to work for the University and be a part of the football program. I couldn't tell just one story, there are too many. So I give you...

The 1960 Season

The 1960 football season was incredible. We ended the season undefeated, winning all of our games except for LSU, which we tied. We also won the SEC and played in the Sugar Bowl against Rice, beating them 14-6. That victory resulted in our being named National Champions, but it was a tough road to get that far.

Ole Miss vs. Arkansas, October 22

We played the Razorbacks in Little Rock. They had a good team and were ready to play. We had a winning record and they were after us, big time.

Arkansas scored first, so it was 7-0 early in the game. We came back in the second half and Jake Gibbs threw a touchdown pass to Ralph "Catfish" Smith, which tied the score.

Late in the game, we drove the ball to Arkansas' 25- or 30-yard line. With only seconds to go, we had to kick a field goal. Allen Green, our fine place kicker, kicked the ball, and it was good. Unfortunately, right before the kick, the referee, Tommy Bell, had blown the ball dead because of the crowd noise. We had to repeat the down. So we lined up and Allen kicked it again. The second kick was good and we won 10-7.

Arkansas contested. They said the ball never went through the goal post. Somebody else said that the second Allen kicked the ball the game was over because the referee's hands went up. It was an unbelievable scene. The crowd poured out of the stands onto the field, and we literally had to fight our way out of the stadium. Arkansas fans still talk about the game we should never have won.

Ole Miss vs. LSU, October 29

The next week we played LSU in Oxford. It was good to be home, especially after the fiasco the week before in Little Rock. We were still pretty bruised and beat up from the game with Arkansas, but we were very excited about playing LSU.

We were behind 6-3, and the end of the game was quickly approaching. We drove down the field the same way we had against Arkansas. With twenty seconds to go, Allen Green again was called to duty. He lined up, kicked a field goal, and made it. We tied the game 6-6, which enabled us to win the SEC.

Two weeks in a row, Allen Green was the pressure man, and two weeks in a row, he came through.

Ole Miss vs. Tennessee, November 12

One of our greatest games was against Tennessee. We had never beaten Tennessee in Knoxville, but we did in 1960. Our fullbacks, Hoss Anderson and Billy Ray Adams, had a great day, and so did Jake Gibbs, our quarterback.

Tennessee played a Wide-Tackle 6 defense and played it as good as, or better, than anyone in the country. Knowing we had to win that game, Coach Vaught devised an offensive game plan that absolutely worked to perfection. We beat the Volunteers 19-6.

After the game, and an unbelievable offensive day, our saying was, "That was the day we put the Wide-Tackle 6 out of business."

Remembering Chucky

I have always known that Ole Miss people were very close, but when I was athletic director, I witnessed how being a part of Ole Miss is really like having an extended family. When Chucky Mullins was injured in the Vanderbilt game in 1989, Ole Miss fans, students and friends in the Southeastern Conference rallied with unrivaled support.

Over one million dollars was donated to Chucky and his family. The University built a house for them in Oxford. Chucky was a real campus hero, even being elected Colonel Rebel by fellow students.

Eggplant Josephine

1 lg. eggplant	*½ T. Worcestershire sauce*
1 8 oz. pgk. mozzarella cheese	*½ stick butter*
1 can or 1 lb. fresh crabmeat	*½ c. Sauterne wine*
Italian spaghetti meat sauce	*2 to 3 T. dry mustard*
2 eggs	*salt and white pepper to taste*
2 c. mayonnaise	

Crabmeat Topping

Melt butter and add wine. Remove any shell fragments from the crabmeat. Add meat to wine and butter. Boil about 6 minutes and set aside.

Italian Meat Sauce

Any spaghetti type sauce is acceptable. Make sure meat is finely ground and smooth. Heat sauce and set aside.

Hollandaise Topping

Beat 2 egg yolks until frothy. Blend in mayonnaise and add Worcestershire. Add salt and white pepper to taste. Add dry mustard (the more mustard, the tangier the topping).

Eggplant

Preheat oven to 450 degrees. Peel and slice eggplant about 3/4 to 1 inch thick. Flour and fry eggplant until slightly brown. Assemble eggplant, crabmeat topping, meat sauce and shredded cheese in shallow pan. Bake until cheese is melted, bubbly and begins to brown. Remove from oven and serve in single slices. Top with heated hollandaise.

Warner Alford
Jackson, Mississippi

Billy Brewer

Position & Years
QB & Defensive Back 1957-59

Nickname
Dog

All SEC 1959
College All-Star Game 1960
SEC Coach of the Year 1990

Amateur Football Award 1993
Team of the Century

The Big Nickel

by Billy Brewer

When I was coaching at Ole Miss, Chucky Mullins and I met a very special person.

I got to the office early that day. I didn't have a secretary, so when the phone rang, I picked it up.

"One moment for the president," an unidentified voice said.

I didn't know if it was the president of a company, another college, or what.

The unidentified voice repeated his opening adding, "One moment for the Office of The President of the United States."

"Yeah, right, and I'm the damn chancellor too."

"No, I'm not kidding, this is the Office of the President of the United States of America, and President George Bush wants to know if you can be in Memphis this morning by 10:30."

I sat up straight and replied, "Yeah, I guess, sure."

He then told me the Secret Service would be doing a security check on me, and I had to be in a certain place at a certain time to go through this procedure. I found this kind of funny, because, as I told the "voice," there really wasn't much to check about me. He agreed, but told me this was protocol.

When I arrived at Baptist Hospital in Memphis, I was frisked, and "checked out." I could hardly wait to tell Chucky what was about to happen, so I immediately started toward his room in intensive care.

"Nickel Back" I began, (we called him Nickel Back, because he was the fifth back we played) "today the Big Nickel is coming to see you!"

He asked, "Who's that?"

I grinned and said, "President George Bush!"

In stunned disbelief he said, "You're kidding."

"That's what I thought too, but he's coming, and he'll be here between 11:30 and 12:00. I'm not sure if I'll be with him or not, but the guy is coming to see you."

I left to go wait at the end of the hall. Before I knew it, the elevator doors opened and out came two guys dressed in black trench coats, Secret Service agents. I looked again and all of a sudden there were three more agents following the two leaders. They were carrying bags, guns I guess.

I walked toward them, but didn't get very far because one of the agents put his arms up to stop me. About that time, President Bush broke through the security surrounding him and extended his hand to me.

"Hi, Billy, how are you doing today?" he asked.

Of course, he had been briefed about who I was, had seen my picture, and knew all about me, but he sure did have a way of putting me at ease. It was like talking to a "regular guy."

I turned to take a step down the hall, but one of the agents put his hands on my chest and said, "You can't go."

The President looked at me and explained, "I'm sorry, but this is how these guys operate."

Neither of us said another word. I stood there and watched the President of the United States, the most revered and respected man in the world, walk down the hall to visit one of our most loved and respected Ole Miss sons.

He stayed with Chucky for about 20 minutes. I don't know what they talked about. But, I can tell you that Chucky was smiling after George Bush left his room, shook my hand and exited the building among high security, stopped traffic and much fanfare.

Judge Ben Guider of Vicksburg suggested the nickname REBELS in 1936. One of five entries submitted to the Southern sports writers for final selection, it was chosen from more than 200 nicknames.

Ham and Biscuits

2 pkgs. sm. party rolls
3 T. poppy seeds
1 sm. grated onion
½ lb. thin-sliced ham

½ lb. Swiss cheese, grated
2 sticks margarine, softened
1 T. Worcestershire sauce
3 T. Gray spicy mustard

Preheat oven to 350 degrees. Cut rolls in half lengthwise. Mix margarine, mustard, poppy seeds, Worcestershire and onion. Spread mixture on both sides of loaf. Lay cheese on bottom. Lay ham slices on top of cheese. Put top layer of rolls back on the cheese/ham/bread layer. Wrap in foil and fold edges to seal. Bake 20 minutes. Slice rolls apart to serve. Can be prepared ahead and frozen. Delicious served hot or cold. Makes 48 finger rolls.

Shrimp and Crab

5 hard boiled eggs, chopped
1 large onion, chopped
12-14 slices white bread, crusts removed and cut into cubes

One day ahead of time, combine the above ingredients. Cover tightly with plastic wrap, and refrigerate over night.

1 6 oz. can crabmeat, chilled and drained
1 6 oz. can shrimp, chilled and drained
1 c. finely chopped celery
1½ c. mayonnaise
1 T. lemon juice
few dashes lemon pepper
salt to taste

Add the above ingredients to mixture the next day. Keep refrigerated. Use as a spread with your favorite crackers. Of course, fresh shrimp or crab can be used instead of canned.

Billy Brewer
Oxford, Mississippi

Johnny Brewer

Position & Years
End 1957 & 1959-60

Nicknames
Stud, Tonto, Jungle,
Leg & Cheyenne

All American 1960
All SEC 1959 & 60
Senior Bowl 1961

All America Bowl 1961
College All-Star Game 1961
Ole Miss Sports Hall of Fame

Dead Ringer

by Johnny Brewer

Our 1956 freshman class won two Sugar Bowls, one Gator Bowl, became SEC champs, was voted the Team of the Decade (1959) and was number one in the nation. I can modestly say we had a pretty good freshman class.

When the varsity played away games, the redshirted team members had to stay on campus and scrimmage against us. We would whip them pretty bad in those games. They had a way to get even though, and that was to make us their freshmen slaves. It was a tradition that freshman football players had to do whatever the varsity requested, and I can assure you some of those things were pretty bad.

For instance, the varsity and freshman dorms were separate and didn't have central heat or air conditioning. Every morning during the winter a particular varsity player would make one of my classmates get up, walk to the varsity dorm and sit on the toilet to warm it up for him.

But most of all, they loved to hit us with paddles made from bed slats and broken baseball bats. One day Butch Kempinska, Aubrey Sanders, and I decided that we were tired of that kind of abuse, so we decided to call Coach Wobble (Davidson) and tell him we were going home if it didn't stop.

What we couldn't decide was who would make the call to Coach Wobble. In the minds of every football player who ever knew him, Coach Wobble had the mystical powers of a minor god. We odd-manned out and I lost. I can't even describe how much I dreaded that call.

I folded a towel into eight layers and put it over the receiver, knowing full well coach would never figure out who was calling him. Ring-g-g-g, ring-g-g-g, and then he picked up. When I finished telling him what we had decided, he said, "Well, Johnny, we'll look into it."

I nearly fainted. I knew he could see through walls, but telephone lines?

Lock 'Em Up

by Johnny Brewer

Richard (Possum) Price, Aubrey Sanders, Butch Kempinska and I were sitting around the dorm one night after supper. It was pretty boring, so we decided to go see a John Wayne cowboy movie playing at the drive-in. Among the four of us, we had just enough money for two of us to get in. No problem. Two of us would just ride in the trunk and sneak in. Since Sanders owned the car, we knew it wouldn't be him, so the rest of us odd-manned out. Possum and I lost.

We headed to the drive-in and right before we got to the bottom of the hill to go in, we stopped and Possum and I crawled into the trunk. It was a tight fit because both of us were pretty big men, and we had eaten a pretty big meal an hour or so earlier. We heard the tires going over the gravel, and then the car stopped at the admission booth. We heard some talking but couldn't understand what was being said.

About that time, the car moved forward, and then we were turning around going out of the drive-in. We hit the highway and drove around for a good while. Then we slowed down and were driving some more. Possum and I didn't know what was going on, but we sure were uncomfortable crammed up in the truck of that car. We had been in there for about 25 minutes.

Then we stopped. We heard two doors slam. Freedom! But Sanders and Kempinska never unlocked the trunk. They were gone at least another 30 minutes. We didn't know what was going on. It seemed an eternity before they came back. I'm a little bit claustrophobic, so I was beginning to panic.

Finally, we heard the engine start. We were driving again, and this time we made it to the drive-in. They opened the trunk to let us out, laughing like they had pulled off the trick of the century.

"What the heck's been going on," we asked.

"They changed the time the movie started, and we thought we'd go downtown to play a little pool while we were waiting," they said.

I guarantee you one thing; that was the last time I ever sneaked into a drive-in.

Steele Bayou Hush Puppies

1 c. self-rising yellow corn meal
¼ c. self-rising flour
1 egg
1 pod jalapeño pepper, finely minced
⅓ lg. bell pepper, finely minced
1 T. Cajun mustard
1 tsp. Worcestershire sauce
½ c. green onions, chopped
½ c. buttermilk
salt and pepper to taste
2 to 3 c. peanut oil

Mix all of the above except peanut oil. Heat peanut oil on medium to medium high heat. Dip a tablespoon in hot peanut oil, then use it to spoon hush puppy mix into hot oil. Rake mix off spoon with fingers, dip spoon in hot oil frequently. Cook to a golden brown. Cook to dark brown if you like them crispy.

Pecan Pie

1 c. dark corn syrup
¾ c. sugar
3 eggs, lightly beaten
3 T. butter

1 tsp. vanilla
1½ c. pecans, broken
unbaked pie shell

Preheat oven to 375 degrees. Boil syrup and sugar together for about 2 minutes. Pour slowly over eggs, stirring well. Add butter, vanilla and nuts. Pour into unbaked pie shell. Bake for 35 to 40 minutes or until done. Hint: When the pie is totally "puffed" across the top, it will be done.

Johnny Brewer
Vicksburg, Mississippi

Allen Brown

Position & Years
Tight End 1962-64

Nickname
Red

All American 1964
Sophomore All SEC 1962
All SEC 1963 & 64
Team Co-Captain 1964

Blue-Gray Game 1964
Senior Bowl 1965
College All-Star Game 1965
Ole Miss Sports Hall of Fame

Right of Center

by Allen Brown

My sophomore year we were playing Vanderbilt at Ole Miss. It was a day game and we were heavily favored.

In the third quarter Coach Vaught sent in a bunch of us sophomores to play. We were a good bit nervous because this was the first game we got to play together.

We all knew our quarterback, sophomore Jimmy Heidel, was really keyed up since he could barely call the play. When we broke huddle, all of us, Ray Beddingfield, center, Bobby Robinson, guard, C.A. Ford, tackle and I, the end, ran to the line of scrimmage.

When Jimmy came to the line and started calling the signal, I just happened to look and noticed he was behind the guard instead of the center.

I hollered at him, "Jimmy, move down, you're under the guard!"

Well, he took me at my word all right. He moved down, but to his right, not his left, and got under C.A. Ford at right tackle. Then he started barking out the signals again!

What Coach Vaught Said:

I've had other quarterbacks do that, but they don't stay long. Jimmy stayed longer than any quarterback I can remember. I knew he was excited, but the guy he got under should have slapped him off. I still think that's funny. I laughed when it happened.

C.M. "Tad" Smith served as athletic director at Ole Miss for 25 years. He retired in 1971. The campus coliseum is named after Smith.

Sweet Beans

1 gal. Bush's Best or Allen's baked beans
3 lbs. ground chuck
2 lbs. bacon
3 lg. onions
1 lg. bell pepper
2 lbs. Cajun style sausage
1½ bottles Bull's Eye regular barbecue sauce

All of the above ingredients will fit into a #10 or #12 Dutch oven. Brown hamburger meat and drain excess grease. Cut bacon into 1 inch strips, brown and drain. Cut onions and bell pepper into pieces and saute until clear. Cut sausage into pieces, brown slightly and drain. ***This next step is very important. Stand can of beans up for fifteen minutes and then open. Drain all the liquid off the beans.*** Put beans in Dutch oven with hamburger meat, bacon, sausage, bell pepper, onions and barbecue sauce. Mix together. Heat beans in oven until warm enough to eat. Don't over cook because you want the beans to stay together. Stir and serve.

Amaretto Dip

1 c. sliced almonds
1 c. powdered sugar
2 8 oz. pkgs. cream cheese, softened
½ c. amaretto

Toast the almonds. Mix with other ingredients. Make a day ahead of time and serve with sliced Granny Smith apples*.

*Slice apples a day ahead of time and refrigerate in pineapple juice to keep from turning brown.

Ole Miss Puppies

1 pkg. Martha White hushpuppy mix
1 medium onion
1 bell pepper
1 egg
1 can diced Rotel Tomatoes
2 T. chopped parsley
salt and pepper
Grease for frying

Chop onion in blender and put in bowl. Chop bell pepper in blender and drain juice off by mashing in a strainer. Add bell pepper to onion. Drain tomatoes, reserving juice, and add to onion and bell pepper. Add chopped parsley and salt and pepper to taste. Mix ingredients. Mixture needs to be thick. You can add juice from tomatoes if you need it. After stirring, let mixture sit five minutes. Put grease in pot or use fish grease and add mixture with teaspoon using only half a teaspoon of mixture per hushpuppy. Let brown on both sides, turning them as they cook and drain on paper towels.

Allen Brown
Ferriday, Louisiana

Allen Brown and Bobby Robinson, (left guard, 1962-64), were suite mates in Miller Hall, the athletic dorm. They were also co-captains of the 1964 team. Le Robinson, Bobby's daughter, met Tim Brown, Allen's son, when they were students at Ole Miss. In 1993 Le and Tim were married. Allen and Bobby agree that they are the only former co-captains and roommates in Ole Miss history whose children have married.

The Charlie Conerly Trophy

The Charlie Conerly Trophy, established by the Mississippi Sports Foundation Inc., is given annually to Mississippi's outstanding college football player. Established in 1996, the award is designed to be Mississippi's equivalent of the Heisman Trophy.

After careful research, criteria for the winner of The Conerly Trophy were established. College players in Mississippi, regardless of their class, player position or school size are eligible. There is no nomination process; 54 voters have an opportunity to vote for whomever they choose. The voters are media representatives, both print and broadcast, from a mixed set of markets around the state. Perian Conerly, wife of Charlie, serves on the selection committee.

The award is an original bronze sculpture, crafted by nationally recognized artist Bruce Brady, a Brookhaven native, who donated his time. The winner receives an exact replica of the original trophy, which is on permanent display in the Mississippi Sports Hall of Fame and Museum. The imagery on the trophy is patterned after a painting of Charlie playing with the New York Giants that Mrs. Conerly especially liked.

The award was named after Charlie Conerly because he was a native Mississippian, an All American at a Mississippi college, a NFL Rookie of the Year, a National Football League MVP and the quarterback of a NFL team that won a world championship. He embodied good character and played great football.

The Conerly family has been intimately involved with setting up the award. From designing and selling the luncheon tickets to planning the menu, their input has been invaluable.

The award is given at a luncheon held in Jackson each December. The first Conerly Trophy was presented by former Republican Vice Presidential candidate, Jack Kemp and ABC Sports commentator, Frank Gifford, both former teammates of Conerly's with the Giants.

Tregnel Thomas, a freshman running back from Delta State University, was the Conerly Trophy's first recipient.

Michael Rubenstein
Executive Director
Miss. Sports Foundation

Charlie Conerly

Position & Years
Tailback 1942 & 1946-47

Nickname
Chunkin' Charlie & Roach

Consensus All American 1947
All SEC 1946 & 47
SEC Back of the Year 1947
SEC Player of the Year 1947
All-Time SEC Team

Team Captain 1947
Distinguished American Award
Team of the Century
Miss. Sports Hall of Fame
Ole Miss Sports Hall of Fame

Reflections

by Perian Conerly

Charlie was really proud that the 1947 Rebels were picked by the press to finish 10th in the 12-school SEC. Of course that was the year Ole Miss won the championship for the first time.

Y.A. Tittle of LSU likes to tell the story of intercepting one of Charlie's passes and streaking toward the goal. He says his belt broke and his pants dropped to his knees, tripping him up. Y.A. swears he would have scored otherwise. Charlie, however, said if it happened, he didn't notice it.

More Reflections

by John Vaught

The first game I coached at Ole Miss was probably the most important of my career. It was in 1947 and we were playing Kentucky whose head coach was Bear Bryant. They were picked to beat us by 14 points.

I had made up my mind that they weren't going to beat us because we had a good solid defense. We also had Charlie Conerly throwing the ball, Barney Poole to catch it and Kayo Dottley as a runner.

All we did that game was let Conerly take a quick three-step drop and hit Barney Poole. Now, once in a while, he'd throw to the wide receiver, but mostly he threw to Barney or Kayo.

The score was tied 7-7 late in the fourth quarter. We let Charlie throw little short passes to Barney and Kayo. Charlie finally hit Barney right over the goal line with a spot pass, but as soon as he caught it, a Kentucky linebacker came up and hit him hard, really hard.

The story went out over the wire that we had tied Kentucky 7-7. But that wasn't true. Barney held on to Charlie's pass and we beat those Wildcats 14-7. It was sure a nice way to start my career as head coach.

Perian's Old-Fashioned Fudge
(new style)

2 c. sugar
2 heaping T. cocoa
2 T. light corn syrup
1 5 ounce can evaporated milk

1 tsp. vanilla
pinch of salt
1 tsp. oleo
pecans, chopped

Mix dry ingredients in a 2 1/2 quart Pyrex measuring bowl with a handle. Add milk and slowly stir out lumps. Add corn syrup and stir. Cook in microwave to soft ball stage.* Test. Add oleo and nuts.

Now set the bowl in a pan of cool water for about 30 minutes.** Beat, then pour into an oleo–greased platter, don't use spray.

*In my 700-watt oven, I cook 4 minutes on high, stir, and cook 4 minutes more.

**Or until the bowl is cool enough for you to hold your hand on the bottom of the bowl.

Perian Conerly
Clarksdale, Mississippi

Need a quick idea for your tailgating picnic? Cover a block of cream cheese with canned crabmeat and cocktail sauce. Serve with your favorite crackers.

Ole Miss selected red and blue as its colors from Harvard's Crimson and Yale's Navy Blue.

Bobby Crespino

Position & Years
Right Halfback 1958-60

Nickname
Pluto

College All Star Game 1961
Senior Bowl 1961
All America Bowl 1961

Miss. Sports Hall of Fame
Ole Miss Sports Hall of Fame

Vardaman Woes

by Bobby Crespino

Being a freshman football player at Ole Miss had some great advantages. The camaraderie we shared was incredible. I made wonderful friends, and played with some of the most outstanding college football players in the country. The enormous amount of time we spent with one another enhanced our commitment to each other, the team and the winning tradition at Ole Miss.

Freshmen lived in Vardaman Hall and the varsity team lived next door in Garland Hall. We figured they must have stayed up nights thinking of ways to drive us crazy, because they hounded us mercilessly.

It was our duty to do everything for them. We'd shine shoes, get them food, wash their cars, and clean their rooms. It was expected of us, and no one dared buck the system. I still remember Sunday nights. They were the worst. It never failed that as soon as we were asleep, the varsity players would burst through the doors, wake us up and make us believe, again, that they were in charge of our lives. They were.

By the time I was a senior, the system had changed. Each varsity member was given a freshman to be his gopher. My freshman was outstanding tackle Jim Dunaway. Jim shined my shoes, got my food, ran errands and cleaned my room.

Nowadays, all of the fun and games we engaged in wouldn't be tolerated. I'm not saying everything we did was right, but I will tell you that when you're all in something together, no matter how humiliating or frustrating it seems at the time, it does bring you closer together. You learn to work together, think together, and stick together through all kinds of adversity.

Maybe that's why the friends I made when I played football are still my friends. We share secrets that keep the bonds strong, and the memories of our playing days at Ole Miss still tug at our heart strings.

Caramel Cake

3 sticks butter

6 eggs

1 tsp. vanilla

4 c. flour

2 c. sugar

1 c. milk

$3^1/_2$ tsp. baking powder

Preheat oven to 375 degrees. Cream butter and sugar. Add eggs, one at a time. Sift flour and baking powder together and add in small amounts with milk and vanilla. Bake until toothpick inserted comes out clean.

Icing

$2^3/_4$ c. sugar

1 stick butter

$^3/_4$ c. milk

1 tsp. vanilla

Caramelize $^3/_4$ cup sugar in saucepan. Mix 2 cups sugar with the milk in another saucepan. Bring to a rolling boil and pour it over the caramelized sugar, stirring constantly. Cook until mixture comes to soft ball stage, about 2 or 3 minutes. Add butter and vanilla, beat to spreading consistency.

Stuffed Eggs with Crab

1 doz. hard boiled eggs, halved
1 6½ oz. can crabmeat, drained and flaked
2 T. melted butter
2 to 3 T. mayonnaise
4 tsp. onion, grated
½ tsp. salt
¼ c. sour cream
4 drops hot sauce
½ tsp. Worcestershire sauce
⅛ tsp. white pepper

Separate egg yolks from whites. Mash yolks and toss with crab-meat. Blend in a mixture of the remaining ingredients. Stuff whites of eggs.

Double Cheese Dip with Bacon

1 c. creamed cottage cheese
6 oz. Gruyere cheese, grated
4 slices bacon, cooked crisp and crumbled
2 T. salad dressing
1 sm. clove garlic, minced
½ tsp. crushed red pepper
2 T. bell pepper, minced
2 T. radishes, chopped

Combine cheeses, bacon, salad dressing, lemon juice, garlic and red pepper. Stir in green pepper and radishes. Chill until ready to serve. Delicious served with raw vegetables.

Bobby Crespino
Macon, Mississippi

There is a valid distinction between
The University and Ole Miss
even though the separate threads
are closely interwoven.

The University
is buildings, trees and people.
Ole Miss
is mood, emotion and personality.
One is physical,
and the other is spiritual.
One is tangible,
and the other intangible.

The University is respected,
but Ole Miss is loved.
The University gives a diploma
and regretfully terminates tenure,
but one never graduates from
Ole Miss.

Frank E. Everett Jr.
B.A. '32, LLB '34

Doug Cunningham

Position & Years
Tailback 1964-66

Nickname
Legs

All SEC 1966
Team Co-Captain 1966

Ole Miss Sports Hall of Fame
Colonel Rebel

Sugar Bowl Signing

by Doug Cunningham

Coach Buster Poole recruited me for Ole Miss. I also was being recruited by State. I was a senior at Louisville High School and had ties to both schools. I also have four sisters, and they wanted me to go to State because it was closer to home. I finally made up my mind I was going to sign with Ole Miss. My signing day was quite an adventure.

Ole Miss called the day before National Signing Day and said they were on their way to Louisville. I went outside on the porch and waited for Coach Poole to arrive. He was going to the Sugar Bowl, so he was driving one of the official cars–a new, stark white Cadillac convertible. The logo on the door read "Official Car of the Sugar Bowl." I was impressed.

He threw me the keys and said, "Son, why don't you take these keys and go out and have yourself a good time?"

He then put me in that car and took me to an alum's house and hid me in the basement. I spent the night at that alum's house. My dad told me that the coaches from State called looking for me all day and half the night, but he told them I was gone. They wanted to know what in the hell was going on and he said he didn't know.

By the time State caught up with me the next day, I was Ole Miss bound. Coach Poole took that Letter of Intent, headed for Baton Rouge and I never saw that pretty, white Cadillac again.

The first Ole Miss football team was organized in 1893 by Dr. A.L. Bondurant, who also served as manager-coach.

Gridley's Lemon Ice Box Pie

Filling

2½ oz. fresh lemon juice
1⅔ c. condensed milk
4 eggs, separated
1 graham cracker ready-made pie crust

In a large bowl, beat eggs yolks well. Add condensed milk and mix well. Pour lemon juice in slowly, mixing continually and thoroughly. Pour filling in pie crust. Set aside.

Meringue

½ c. sugar
dash of salt

4 egg whites
¼ tsp. vanilla

Preheat oven to 350 degrees. Pour egg whites in mixing bowl. Beat on medium speed until they begin to stiffen. Turn mixer to high speed. Slowly add salt and sugar. Add vanilla and continue beating until sugar is dissolved completely and meringue forms stiff peaks. Spread evenly over pie making sure meringue is not too high. Place in oven to brown meringue. Cool completely.

Doug Cunningham
Jackson, Mississippi

Sausage Balls

2 c. biscuit mix
1 lb. hot or mild sausage
1 lb. mild or sharp cheddar, grated

Combine all ingredients. Mix thoroughly with hands. Roll into walnut size balls. Bake for 10 to 15 minutes. Drain on paper towels. Cool and store in plastic bags in refrigerator. Great hot too.

Eagle Day

Position & Years
Quarterback 1953-55

Nickname
Eagle

All SEC 1954 & 55
All South 1954
Cotton Bowl MVP 1956

Hula Bowl 1956
Miss. Sports Hall of Fame
Ole Miss Sports Hall of Fame

Bang the Drum Slowly

by Eagle Day

When I was a freshman at Ole Miss, I was in ROTC. During this class I spent a great deal of time learning army terms and carrying an M-1 Rifle, which I hated.

Well, I had a friend who was a captain and also headed up the ROTC band. Knowing full well that a drum was lighter than a rifle, I asked him if he could get me transferred to the band. Even though I couldn't play or read a note of music, he got me a transfer and a small drum.

I started beating on that drum and burst the head. He gave me another one, and I burst that one too. Finally, the captain came over and said, "Eagle, my budget won't allow you to play that type of drum. Try this one."

"This one" was a big bass drum. He told me to beat it one, one, one, one, one and repeat it. It didn't take me long to catch on to that beat, and before long I was really good at it.

About two months later the captain told us we were to parade in review with the troops in front of the 3rd army general. When the day came, we lined up on the field ready for action. When the captain gave the command, we started. There I was beating one, one, one, one, one, never letting up until we had finished.

After the review was over, the captain came up to me smiling and said, "Eagle, you did a great job."

"What do you mean?" I asked.

He said, "Your cadence was great. The march was perfect."

I asked him to explain what he meant.

"Your cadence on the drum is what the troops marched by," he explained.

I know I turned pale. I thought I was going to have a heart attack. It never occurred to me that I was responsible for the entire unit keeping in step. I was just out there having a great time and doing whatever I could to get away from that M-1 Rifle.

As You Were

by Eagle Day

Everyday after ROTC I went to football practice. A freshman, I was flattered I made the varsity squad and got to run a few offensive plays.

As quarterback, I had to call the formation, play and snap count, then break the huddle, go to the line of scrimmage and recognize the defense. If I thought the play would go, I'd call the snap count and hand off. If I didn't think it would go, it was my responsibility to change it.

When I got to the line of scrimmage, I saw that the play I called wouldn't work against the defense I was looking at, so I wanted to change it.

I yelled, "Red 94!" (red was the change of color and 94 was the play).

Then I realized that we didn't have a 94 play and I didn't know how to change that, so I yelled out in the most military voice I could muster, "As you were!"

Everybody started laughing and falling to the ground. I thought Coach Vaught would never get up. He really got a kick out of my army lingo.

Ole Miss has produced 23 Rhodes Scholars, a total which ranks first in Mississippi and 10th among American Public Universities. Of the 23 Scholars, four are former Rebel football players: Richard Beckett (1907), Louis M. Jiggitts (1919), Myers McDougal (1926) and Robert Childres (1958).

The Eagle Burger

1½ lbs. ground round   *garlic salt*
½ c. barbecue sauce   *coarse-ground black pepper*

Roll meat into four patties. Sprinkle with garlic salt and pepper. Put on the grill and turn several times while cooking, but do not press as you will lose the juices. Five minutes before they are done, spread the barbecue sauce on each side and continue to cook until ready for buns.

This recipe has made and kept many friends—E.D.

Yum Yum Salad

1 pkg. lemon gelatin
1 8 oz. carton non-dairy whipped topping, thawed
1 medium can crushed pineapple, drained
1 c. mild, fancy shredded cheddar cheese
1 c. pecans, chopped

Dissolve gelatin in one cup boiling water. Set aside to cool. When gelatin is partially congealed, beat with electric mixer on low speed until foamy. Add whipped topping, pineapple, cheese and pecans. Put in dish and store covered in the refrigerator for several hours. Cut in squares and serve.

Eagle Day
Jackson, Mississippi

51

Kenny Dill

Position & Years
Center 1961-63

All American 1963

All SEC 1963

Team Co-Captain 1963

SEC Lineman of the Year 1963

Challenge Bowl 1964

Distinguished American Award

Team of the Century

Ole Miss Sports Hall of Fame

Still Makes Me Laugh

by Kenny Dill

In 1961 we were playing State in Starkville. Our offensive team was near the State goal line. The quarterback called a trap play. About that time, one of our guards asked the quarterback to call another play. He then explained that Johnny Baker, a State defensive end, was "killing" him with his forearm when he went to block him on that particular trap play. I knew Johnny and he was wicked with his forearm. I was dying of laughter at that request.

Chattanooga came to Oxford for our 1961 matchup. They had a player from my hometown of West Point by the name of Carey Henley. He was a running back and their star player.

Our coaches assigned two linebackers to him on every play, whether he had the ball or not. Coach Vaught had told us if we stopped Henley, we stopped Chattanooga.

During the first quarter I was on the field with Henley. I told him to find a way to keep from taking the ball on every play. I also advised him to fall, every time, after the first hit. He didn't take my advice and had to leave the game in the second half–minus his front teeth.

The 1962 Tennessee game in Knoxville was a great one. We were barely ahead, but gaining ground. During a time-out, a former UT player came out on the field, slipped up behind Chuck Morris, our safety, and knocked him down with an umbrella.

Both benches cleared for a big fight. We won the fight and the football game 19-6.

We were in a pre-game team meeting at the hotel before the LSU game in 1963. Coach Vaught called me outside and asked me if I had the team ready to play.

"Coach, I haven't been able to eat for two days because of the butterflies in my stomach. I think everybody is ready," I replied.

Thank goodness we were ready. Whaley Hall blocked a quick

kick on the first series. Stan Hindman made the long run and pushed Joe Labruzzo out at one-yard line. LSU had to settle for a field goal, the only points they scored all night. We won 37-3.

Doc Knight

by Kenny Dill

Many Ole Miss fans didn't know how much our trainer, Wesley "Doc" Knight, meant to us. He was a real motivator to the players. He was also a father away from home.

He would give us pep talks before all games and lead us in prayer. He always told us that if we had the faith of a mustard seed, we could move mountains. Whenever I hear that quote, I always think of Doc Knight.

He was a winner in every sense of the word. Doc Knight sure loved Ole Miss.

Beef Tenderloin

1 4 lb. beef tenderloin
¼ c. lemon juice
¼ c. salad oil
1 tsp. black pepper
1 tsp. of your favorite herb

2 T. MSG
1 tsp. garlic powder
¼ tsp. mace
1 tsp. powdered horseradish

Mix the lemon juice and oil. Marinate the tenderloin in this mixture. Refrigerate overnight. Before cooking, pour juices off meat and mix all other ingredients in the reserved juice. Rub mixture over the tenderloin and bake at 450 degrees for 45 minutes for rare, one hour for well done.

Potato Salad

6 medium red potatoes
4 boiled eggs
1 c. celery, chopped
1 dill pickle, diced
1/4 to 1/2 c. onion, chopped

2 tsp. salt
1 tsp. pepper
1/4 tsp. garlic powder
2 T. mustard
1/2 c. mayonnaise

Boil potatoes and mash. Cut eggs into small pieces and mix with mashed potatoes. Add celery, onions, pickle, salt, pepper and garlic powder. Add mustard and mix thoroughly. Add mayonnaise and mix well.

Dewberry Cobbler

1 stick butter, melted
1 c. sugar
3/4 c. plain flour
2 T. baking powder

pinch of salt
3/4 c. milk
2 c. dewberries or blackberries

Preheat oven to 350 degrees. Mix all ingredients, except butter, in a bowl. Pour into a baking dish and cover with butter. Bake for 30 minutes.

Blonde Brownies

2 c. flour
2 tsp. baking powder
1/4 tsp. salt
1 stick butter or margarine

2 c. packed brown sugar
2 eggs
1 tsp. vanilla
1 c. chopped nuts

Preheat oven to 350 degrees. Mix flour, salt and baking powder. Melt butter, remove from heat and stir in sugar. Add eggs and vanilla, mix well. Stir dry ingredients and nuts into sugar mixture. Spread in 13x9x2 baking pan. Bake 20-25 minutes.

Kenny Dill
West Point, Mississippi

John "Kayo" Dottley

Position & Years
Fullback 1947-50

Nickname
Kayo

All American 1949	Ole Miss Hall of Fame
All SEC 1949 & 50	Colonel Rebel
All South 1949 & 50	Team of the Century
College All-Star Game 1951	Miss. Sports Hall of Fame
Senior Bowl 1951	Ole Miss Sports Hall of Fame

Love At First Sight

by John "Kayo" Dottley

One afternoon a big, long, black Buick drove up to the McGehee (Arkansas) Playground and Tennis Courts. A giant of a man, Coach Buster Poole, stepped out and asked my buddy, Spike Ford, where he could find a boy named Kayo Dottley.

Spike pointed me out and he came over, "When you get through with your game, can I talk to you?" he asked.

"Yes sir, what about?" I asked.

"Well, son, about coming to play football at Ole Miss."

"Where's Ole Miss?" I quizzed.

After the tennis game, he invited me to drive his car "somewhere" we could talk. I drove all over McGehee waving and honking at everyone I knew. Heck, that car was bigger than my house.

Coach Poole and I talked about everything. I liked him immediately. I thanked him for coming but told him I was either going to Arkansas or Alabama. I also told him I was going to meet Bear Bryant, head coach at Kentucky. He nodded and then asked to meet my parents.

After meeting, he asked my dad to bring me to Ole Miss. Dad told him we were planning a visit to Alabama in two weeks and would stop in Oxford to meet the new head football coach, John Vaught.

On the way to Alabama we stopped at Ole Miss. We were supposed to be at the Coach's office at 11:00. We intentionally got to the campus early to look around by ourselves. Right then and there I fell in love with Ole Miss; it was love at first sight.

We finally went to meet Coach Vaught and some other coaches.

They asked me to go see the facilities at the stadium. They then invited me to put on equipment and "run around." Little did I realize I was being given a try-out (legal in those days).

When we got to Alabama, we found out that Red Drew had taken the head coaching job, and Frank Thomas, who had been recruiting me, was leaving. This changed everything. I lost interest in Alabama. Then I found out that freshmen couldn't play varsity in the Southwest Conference, so I ruled out Arkansas.

My meeting with Coach Bryant was great. He convinced me

Arkansas boys needed to stick together and I should come to Kentucky to play. It seemed like a good idea to me.

It was time for graduation and prom and I still had not signed a scholarship. I told both coaches I didn't know what to do. The Tuesday night I graduated, Coaches Vaught and Bryant were sitting in the audience.

When the ceremony was over both said I had to make up my mind. Coach Vaught said Ole Miss was going to have a summer practice for freshmen and it was imperative I attend. I promised both an answer "shortly."

The following Friday night was prom. About 1:30 or 2:00 a.m., I walked in the house. There sat my parents, Coach Vaught, Ole Miss alum Tommy Turner and my packed suitcase. Vaught said, "Son, we're going to Ole Miss, are you ready?"

I said, "I don't know."

He said, "I'm going, your clothes are going and your Momma wants you to go."

Right then and there we loaded in that big, long, black Buick and headed to Oxford. I was practicing football the next day.

The ride up that night, talking to Coach Vaught and Mr. Turner gave me the assurance I had made the right decision.

Ole Miss provided me so many opportunities. I was able to play football for the greatest coaching staff of all time, graduate with a Master's degree in four years, be elected Colonel Rebel, play pro ball and even marry a cheerleader.

What Coach Vaught said:

Kayo surprised people with his outside running. We didn't have much outside running until he got here. Just to look at him, you'd think he was awkward, but when he was running, he was rhythm in motion. He had a beautiful stride.

I took a lot of pride in having him here at Ole Miss. I also took a lot of pride in the fact that I signed him myself. I made the trip and brought him up here in my own car. Getting him to Ole Miss really helped turn our program around.

Muffuletta Sandwich

1 loaf muffuletta bread
2 T. melted butter
dash of oregano
1/2 c. olive oil
4 slices salami
4 slices bologna

pepperoni (optional)
4 slices mozzarella cheese
4 slices Swiss cheese
4 slices American cheese
Italian olive mix

Cut muffuletta bread in half horizontally. Brush with butter, then with olive oil on inside of bread. Sprinkle oregano on top of oil. Next layer meats and cheeses. Brush top of bread with melted butter. Wrap in foil and bake at 350 degrees for 20 minutes or until cheese melts. Remove from oven and spread Italian mix over the melted cheese. Cut into fourths. Serve hot or cold. Serves 4.

To take to your picnic hot, remove from the oven, keep wrapped in foil, roll in newspaper and seal in a brown bag. Add the Italian mix right before serving.

Cindy's Rich Butter Cookies

1 c. butter
1 1/2 c. sugar
1 egg
1 tsp. vanilla

2 1/2 c. flour
1 tsp. baking soda
1 tsp. cream of tarter
1/4 tsp. salt

Preheat oven to 375 degrees. Cream butter. Gradually add sugar, creaming until fluffy. Add unbeaten egg and vanilla. Beat well. Sift together dry ingredients. Blend with creamed mixture. Drop by teaspoons onto cookie sheet. Bake 8 minutes. The secret to these cookies is not to over cook. They may not appear to be done after 8 minutes, but remove from oven anyway.

I can't wait to tailgate just to get Cindy McRight's cookies—K.D.

John "Kayo" Dottley
Vicksburg, Mississippi

University of Mississippi Alma Mater

"Way down south in Mississippi,

There's a spot that ever calls,

Where among the hills enfolded,

Stand old Alma Mater's halls.

Where the trees lift high their branches

To the whispering Southern breeze,

There Ole Miss is calling, calling

To our hearts fond memories."

Doug Elmore

Position & Years
Quarterback 1959-61

Nickname
Snake

All American 1961
All SEC 1961
Academic All America, 1961
Academic All SEC 1961

All America Bowl 1962
Team Co-Captain 1961
Miss. Sports Hall of Fame
Ole Miss Sports Hall of Fame

Momma Said

by Doug Elmore

Thank God Ole Miss found me. By the end of my senior year, I hadn't heard from anybody about playing college ball. I was from Reform, Alabama, 28 miles from Columbus, Mississippi, and attended a small high school. Luckily, my team was selected to play in the Turkey Bowl and Coach John Cain was there scouting.

My brother, J.T., was my coach and one day he got a call from Coach Cain inviting us up to the spring game. Of course, we accepted. Until I went to Oxford for that visit, I had never been west of Columbus. The visit went well, and Cain offered me a scholarship. I eagerly accepted.

My mom, dad and brother took me to Ole Miss to start my first semester. When we pulled up in front of the Athletic Dorm, the first two people I saw were Jackie Simpson and Gene Hickerson. They were juniors or seniors and two of the biggest people I had ever seen in my whole life. They were just hanging out in front of the dorm, leaning on cars, trying to intimidate the incoming freshmen. They were doing a good job of it.

About that time, Bob Benton came out of the dorm with his head shaved, which automatically told me he was a freshman. Well, hell, he was bigger than the other two guys. He had big arms and an 18 inch neck. I was 6 feet 4 inches tall and weighed about 165 pounds. Thank heavens for the training table.

My mother was sitting in the back seat of the car taking it all in and finally said, "Son, I don't know whether we ought to leave you up here or not."

I almost agreed with her that I maybe should go back home with them. I didn't unpack for a couple of weeks, because I didn't know how long I could stand to be around those big guys.

My arrival at Ole Miss was scary, but my days at Ole Miss were the best.

Cupcake Brownies

4 squares semi-sweet chocolate
2 sticks oleo
1 c. plain unsifted flour
4 eggs

1³/₄ c. sugar
2 tsp. vanilla
2 c. pecans, chopped (optional)

Preheat oven to 325 degrees. Melt the chocolate and oleo in a double boiler. Mix flour and sugar together. Add eggs, one at a time, stirring as little as possible. Add vanilla and chocolate mixture. Stir in pecans. Pour mixture into paper baking cups in muffin tins and bake 25 minutes.

Butter Pecan Turtle Squares

Crust

2 c. flour
1 c. firmly packed brown sugar

1 stick oleo

Caramel Layer

²/₃ c. oleo
¹/₂ c. brown sugar

1 to 1¹/₂ c. whole pecans
1 c. milk chocolate chips

Preheat oven to 350 degrees. Combine crust ingredients and pat firmly into a 13x9x2 pan. Sprinkle pecans over unbaked crust. Prepare caramel layer by cooking butter and brown sugar over medium heat, stirring constantly. Pour caramel layer over nuts. Bake 18 to 22 minutes until caramel layer is bubbly and crust is golden. Remove from oven and immediately sprinkle chocolate chips over top. Let chips melt slightly then lightly swirl, do not spread.

Doug Elmore
Jackson, Mississippi

Ken Farragut

Position & Years
Center 1947-50
Linebacker

Nickname
Dynamite

All American Hon. Mention
Team Captain 1950

College All-Star Game
Ole Miss Sports Hall of Fame

The Tooth Fairy

by Ken Farragut

Anyone who played under Coach John Vaught would agree on two statements. One, he was never at a loss for words, and two, he had an uncanny sense of humor. I think that's what made our practices fun, yet effective.

One particular hot, humid Mississippi day we were having a pretty intense scrimmage. As the weather got hotter so did the competition. We were hitting hard, sweating so badly our hands could barely hold onto the ball and feeling the pressure to keep our positions on the team.

I was finally taken out for a rest and my replacement, Charles "Bubba" Bidgood was sent in to snap the ball. Before I knew it, Bubba had been kicked in the mouth (we didn't wear face masks in those days). He quickly put his hand up to his mouth and got a handful of teeth and blood.

Coach Vaught went over to Bubba, reached in his own mouth, pulled out his whole upper bridge and said to Bubba in the most Jack Benny deadpan you've ever seen, "Don't worry about losing your teeth son, you can borrow these anytime."

Talk about a way to break the ice, hell, even Bubba couldn't help but laugh.

Until October 16, 1982, Ole Miss played all of its home games at Hemingway Stadium. At that time, John Howard Vaught's name was added. It is now called Vaught-Hemingway Stadium.

Since I live in Pennsylvania, I only get to Oxford for one or two games a season. Jane and I like to tailgate in the den when we watch the Rebels play on television. This is one of our favorite halftime main courses.

Lobster Stuffed Tenderloin

4 to 7 lbs. whole beef tenderloin
2 4 oz. fresh lobster tails
1 T. melted butter
1 stick unmelted butter
1½ tsp. lemon juice

½ c. sliced green onions
½ c. dry white wine
⅛ tsp. garlic, crushed
4 slices bacon

For garnish: ¼ to ½ lb. whole mushrooms and 12 sprigs parsley

Preheat oven to 425 degrees. Cut tenderloin lengthwise to within 1/2 inch of bottom. Fold two sides open, butterfly fashion. Submerge lobster tails in just enough boiling salt water to cover them. Return to boiling, reduce heat and simmer 5 to 7 minutes. Drain and remove lobster from shells so that tails remain intact. Cut in half lengthwise. Place them end-to-end inside the butterflied beef. Combine melted butter and lemon juice; pour over lobster. Close meat around lobster and tie tenderloin at 1 to 2 inch intervals with kitchen twine. Place on rack in shallow roasting pan with bacon slices on top. Roast 12 to 15 minutes per pound to yield rare doneness.

Wine Sauce

In a saucepan, cook onions in remaining butter over very low heat until tender, stirring frequently. Add wine and crushed garlic, then heat, continuing to stir.

To serve, slice tenderloin and spoon wine sauce over it. Garnish with mushrooms and parsley. Serves 6.

Mississippi Mud Cake

1 c. oil
$\frac{1}{3}$ c. cocoa
4 eggs
$1\frac{3}{4}$ c. sugar

$1\frac{1}{2}$ c. self-rising flour
2 tsp. vanilla
2 c. pecans, chopped
1 pkg. miniature marshmallows

Preheat oven to 300 degrees. Mix ingredients, except marshmallows, and bake in a 9x13 pan for 30 to 45 minutes. Cover with marshmallows as soon as removed from oven.

Frosting

$1\frac{1}{2}$ sticks margarine
1 T. vanilla
1 box powdered sugar

$\frac{1}{3}$ c. cocoa
$\frac{1}{2}$ c. evaporated milk
$\frac{1}{2}$ c. pecans, chopped

Mix all ingredients. Do not cook. Pour over cake while it's still warm.

Roasted Party Pecans

1 c. unsalted pecan halves
1 T. olive or salad oil

1 T. Worcestershire sauce

Preheat oven to 275 degrees. Toss the pecans with oil and Worcestershire. Roast in a shallow baking pan for 30 minutes, stirring often. Drain on paper towels and then sprinkle with salt. Store in air tight container.

Ken Farragut
Flourtown, Pennsylvania

Taking your grill to the Grove? Don't forget the charcoal and lighter fluid.

Mike Fitzsimmons

Position & Years
Defensive Tackle 1983-86

Nickname
Fitz

All American Hon. Mention
All SEC 1986
Team Co-Captain 1986
SEC Player of the Week

Memphis Player of the Year
Hinds County Chapter
   Most Dedicated Player Award

Billy's Billy Bob's

by Mike Fitzsimmons

Coach Billy Brewer was some kind of motivator. He was kind of laid-back and had a lot of country in him, but he also had an incredible way of relating to his players. He was one heck of a man and a great coach.

His first year at Ole Miss, which was my freshman year, we started off the season horribly. By the time we went to play TCU in Fort Worth, we were 1-5 and needing desperately to win.

We boarded the plane Friday and landed safely. Buses were there to meet us, and as we were driving along, everybody was really excited because of a rumor circulating among us. We had heard that if we won the game, Coach Brewer had a big surprise for us. All the buzz was about what the surprise might be.

During practice Friday afternoon, there was more talk and more excitement. Everyone was wondering what we were going to get from Coach if we won the game. Finally, the seniors found out and let the rest of us in on the secret. Coach Brewer was going to let us stay overnight in Fort Worth instead of flying right back to Oxford. Not only that, he was going to take us partying at what we had heard was the biggest bar in the world, Billy Bob's.

Other than winning the game, all most of us could talk about was how we were going to get i.d. cards to get into the bar and order drinks. I mean this bar was supposed to be one and a half miles long, full of music and pretty women, and a romping, stomping good time. We were so fired up. We knew we had to win so we could get to Billy Bob's Bar that night.

We beat TCU 20-7. We were in the dressing room getting cleaned up after the game and talking about the fun we were about to have. We couldn't stand the wait another minute. Finally Coach told us it was time to load up. We all gave each other a little wink, knowing he was about to spring the big surprise on us.

We got on the bus and Coach Brewer had the driver go out of the way, away from the air strip, right onto the interstate. We looked to the left and there sat Billy Bob's. Everybody started cheering and getting restless. We were about to pop right out of our seats. (contd.)

Billy's Billy Bob's (contd.)

About that time Coach stood up, said something to the bus driver, then turned to us and said, "I told you fellas if you won this game I'd take you by Billy Bob's, and there it goes."

We went by all right–at 65 miles per hour.

If you live in or around the Memphis area, or happen to be passing through, be sure to catch Mike on radio station, WREC, A.M. 600, for Sports Line. The show is hosted by Dave Woloshin, the voice of the University of Memphis Tigers. During football season, Mike is on the air with him every Wednesday and Friday afternoon from 5:00 until 7:00. He welcomes call-ins, especially from Ole Miss fans.

Mock Quesadillas

1 8 oz. pkg. cream cheese
1 8 oz. carton sour cream
4 green onions, chopped
1 sm. can chopped jalapeños

1 sm. can chopped black olives
1 taco seasoning packet
3 pkgs. sm. soft tortillas

Mix all ingredients except tortillas. Spread a very small portion of the mixture on the tortilla, then layer another tortilla on top, spread more mixture and top it off with a final tortilla. Cut into 4 to 8 wedges. Repeat until mixture is gone. This will make quite a bit. Serve with fresh salsa for dipping. Can be made with fat-free cream cheese and sour cream.

Italian Beef

4 to 5 lb. roast
salt and pepper to taste
2 jars mild or hot pepperoncini with juice

Preheat oven to 325 degrees. Cover roast with above ingredients. Cook until meat falls apart, about 4 hours. Shred meat and serve on hoagie rolls. May be cooked in a Crock-Pot overnight.

Mike Fitzsimmons
Eads, Tennessee

Fried Chicken Wings
with Dipping Sauce

Chicken Wings

24 chicken wings   *2 tsp. salt*
1 c. oil   *1 tsp. black pepper*
1½ c. flour

Melt oil in frying pan. Mix flour with seasonings. Dip chicken wings in flour mixture. Fry until brown.

Dipping Sauce

2 cans cranberry sauce   *⅔ c. horseradish*
4 tsp. salt   *2 c. sour cream*
2 tsp. pepper sauce

Mash cranberry sauce. Add seasonings and horseradish. Mix thoroughly. Chill.

Charlie Flowers

Position & Years
Fullback 1957-59

Nickname
Big Car

All American 1959
All SEC 1958 & 59
All South 1959
Team Co-Captain 1959
Academic All American 1959

Academic All SEC 1958 & 59
Team of the Decade 1959
Team of the Century
Miss. Sports Hall of Fame
Ole Miss Sports Hall of Fame

Kent's Kick

by Charlie Flowers

In the last game of the 1958 season against Mississippi State, I kind of separated my shoulder. I didn't want anybody to know about it because we were going to Jacksonville to play Florida in the Gator Bowl, and I didn't want to sit on the sidelines.

At one point in the game I was blocking for our halfback, Kent Lovelace, and because my shoulder was still giving me problems, and I couldn't use it, I hit head-on with one of the guys from Florida. When we hit, he spun me around and Kent Lovelace kicked me in the face. That kick broke my nose, depressed my cheekbone, and tore the retina in my eye. I was hurt really badly.

They dragged me, moaning and groaning to the sidelines. I was just lying there being attended by Doc Varner, our team doctor. Every now and then Coach Vaught would ask him if I could go back in, and the answer was always the same: No.

At halftime they took me to the dressing room where Lovelace said to Vaught, "Coach, you're going to have to get Flowers out of here, he's making all of us sick." I guess my teammates didn't like the sight of blood or sounds of pain.

I must have passed out, because after the half, I kind of came to, and Doc Varner was starring down at me. You have to understand something. Doc Varner was the most intense Rebel fan you have ever seen. He rarely missed a practice and never a game. He bled red and blue.

As I awakened, I could hear the cheering and everything, and there was no one in the dressing room but Doc and me. I looked at him and said, "Doc, I'm going to die."

"No you're not. You're hurt, but you're not going to die," he promised.

"Yes I am too," I insisted.

"Why do you think you're going to die?" he asked.

To which I replied, "Because you're in here with me and Ole Miss is out there playing football. If I were just hurt a little bit, you wouldn't be in here with me." (contd.)

73

Through the years, every time Lovelace and I talked about that incident, he'd tell me; "The only reason you got hurt is because you couldn't block. If you had gotten out of the way, I'd have scored."

There's one more tidbit you have to know. That game was one of the few that my parents couldn't get to, but it was being televised, and they were at home watching. The network was experimenting with putting microphones on the refs so fans could hear what they were saying.

Well, when Lovelace kicked me, the ref leaned over to see if I was okay. As he bent over me, I looked up at Kent and said, "Man, you've killed me."

Of course, the ref's mike picked it up, and my parents went crazy. They started calling the press box, the dressing room, and the hospitals. They thought I *really* was dead, and to tell you the truth, for a minute there, I did too.

Charlie Flowers drove a small car that his teammates loved making fun of. Little did they know his father owned a funeral home. One Sunday night, he returned to school driving his father's hearse. From that day forward, he was called Big Car.

Texas Sheet Cake

Cake

2 c. flour	4 T. cocoa
2 c. sugar	1 c. water
1 tsp. baking soda	2 eggs, beaten
½ tsp. salt	½ c. buttermilk
2 sticks margarine	1 tsp. vanilla

Preheat oven to 350 degrees. Put flour, sugar, baking soda and salt in a bowl. Mix margarine, cocoa and water in a sauce pan. Bring to a boil. Pour over flour mixture. Add eggs, buttermilk and vanilla. Bake on edged cookie sheet for 15 to 20 minutes or until done.

Icing

1 stick margarine	1 box powdered sugar
4 T. cocoa	vanilla extract
4 T. buttermilk	nuts (optional)

Bring first three ingredients to a boil. Add powdered sugar and vanilla extract to taste. Add nuts if desired. Put on warm cake.

Charlie Flowers
Atlanta, Georgia

Stuffed Celery

1 sm. avocado	1 tsp. onion, finely chopped
1½ tsp. lemon juice	6 oz. crabmeat
1 T. mayonnaise	celery sticks
red pepper to taste	

Peel and pit the avocado. Cut into quarters. Combine with the lemon juice. Coarsely mash the avocado. Stir in mayonnaise and onion. Add crabmeat. Toss gently. Stuff into celery sticks. Garnish with red pepper.

John Fourcade

Position & Years
Quarterback 1978-81

Nickname
Mississippi Gambler

All SEC 1979 & 80
Team Co-Captain 1981
Sophomore All SEC 1979
Sophomore of the Year 1979
John Vaught Award 1982

Senior Bowl MVP Offense
Who's Who 1981
Colonel Rebel
Ole Miss Hall of Fame 1981

Last Dance–Last Chance

by John Fourcade

I'll never forget my last college football game. The 1981 Egg Bowl was being played in Jackson. Steve Sloan was our coach and Emory Bellard was at the helm for Mississippi State.

As usual emotions were running high on both sides of the stadium. Fans and players were competing for bragging rights, and we wanted the victory. The weather was sunny, and we took an early lead. Things were going just like we had planned. But then...

Toward the end of the game, State had the ball and it was third and one, maybe two. Believe it or not–and we couldn't believe it–Emory Bellard decided to kick a field goal on third down. We were in shock. All they had to do was run one more down, then kick the field goal, and they would win the game. But wonders never cease. They did kick the field goal, made it and went up by four points.

With 37 seconds to go, they kicked off to us. It was a squib kick and we got the ball on about our own 30-yard line. I threw two passes, both to Michael Harmon, to get down field to about their 30-yard line. We were all so fired up, we knew we had a chance to win the game.

With 14 seconds left, we called a time-out to discuss our play. We knew all we had time to do was get in the end zone, so we ended up calling a pass play, a post corner route to Michael again. He ran it, I threw and the ball got intercepted in the end zone.

Well, before you know it, the ref throws a flag, PASS INTER-FERENCE against Mississippi State! The entire stadium went crazy. State and Ole Miss fans were yelling, screaming and who knows what else. It was unbelievable. We were ecstatic, they were totally ticked off.

We get the ball with the penalty, and the ref puts it on the 2-yard line. We break huddle and as we're walking to the line of scrimmage, a Mississippi State player gets mad and kicks the football. BAM, another flag! And guess what, all of a sudden, we're a yard closer to the end zone.

State now calls a time-out to get calmed down and decide how they are going to keep us from scoring. We headed to our sideline

77

to talk things over with Coach Sloan.

The last words I told him were, "I'm going to keep this football, I'm going to score the touchdown and we're going to end this game and my career right here. I *want* the football!"

We got back in the huddle and I called a formation that we lined up totally wrong. They should have had us. We should have had two tight ends but ended up with one. We spread everybody out which was really a messed up offensive formation, but in our excitement, we didn't even realize it.

We ran 38 Option. I had the option to hand it off, keep it or pitch it. Well I knew doggone well I was going to keep the football.

I faked it to Andre "Hammerhead" Thomas over the top, and just about everybody on the State team tackled him. I just stepped around, walked into the end zone and held the ball over my head.

THE GAME ENDS. WE WIN! The final score was 21-17.

That's how I ended my career at Ole Miss, with the winning touchdown to beat Mississippi State.

 Ole Miss boasts 10 members in the National Football Hall of Fame: Bruiser Kinard (1951 Charter Member), Charlie Conerly (1965), John L. Cain (1973), Barney Poole (1974), John H. Vaught (1979), Doug Kenna (1984), Thad "Pie" Vann (1987), Archie Manning (1989), Parker Hall (1991) and Jake Gibbs (1995).

Chicken Casserole

4 to 6 chicken breasts, boiled in salt water and diced
2 6 oz. pkgs. wild rice, with seasonings
1 c. chicken broth
1 can cream of celery soup
2 cans French-style green beans, drained
1 can water chestnuts, drained and diced
1 c. mayonnaise
1 sm. can sliced mushrooms, drained

Preheat oven to 350 degrees. Mix all ingredients and pour into a casserole dish. Cover and cook for 50 minutes. Uncover and continue cooking for 10 more minutes.

Bourbon Balls

2½ c. vanilla wafers, crushed
1 c. pecans
1 c. powdered sugar

2 T. cocoa
2 T. light corn syrup
½ c. bourbon

Grind wafers and pecans in food processor. Mix with sugar and cocoa. Stir the syrup into the bourbon and pour over dry ingredients. Mix until moistened and shape into balls. Roll in powdered sugar. Store in air tight containers.

John Fourcade
Harvey, Louisiana

Bobby Franklin

Position & Years
Quarterback 1957-1959

Nicknames
Waxie & One Shot

All SEC 1958	College All-Star Game 1960
MVP Gator Bowl 1958	All Time Sugar Bowl Team
MVP Cotton Bowl 1958	Distinguished American Award
MVP Sugar Bowl 1960	Ole Miss Sports Hall of Fame

A Block Will Cost Ya Fifty
by Bobby Franklin

In 1958 we played Arkansas in Little Rock. It was one of the toughest games we had played all year. When the buzzer went off, we had won the game 14-12. We were beaten up pretty badly.

I ended up in the hospital with a cracked rib and didn't return to Oxford until Sunday morning. My buddy, Charlie Flowers, was laying on the field bleeding like a stuck hog, and Larry Grantham also was hurt. The whole game was brutal.

I had left the field when a fan made his way down and handed Charlie Flowers $100. "Give this to Franklin. He scored both touchdowns today, and I want him to have it," he said.

The next afternoon, we were all at the field house and I saw Charlie. He gave me $50 and told me a fan had sent it by him. I was happy to get it. A few days later, one of my buddies asked me if I had gotten the $100 Charlie had for me.

"A hundred dollars? He only gave me fifty," I said.

So we found Charlie and I asked him where my other $50 was.

"Well, hell, man, I blocked for you, so I get half of it," he replied.

Now, who was I to argue with that logic?

Kentucky Pain

by Bobby Franklin

Warner Alford swears I did this, but I don't remember at all. He says it happened when we were playing Kentucky at Commonwealth Stadium. I do remember that right behind our bench was a tall and ominous brick wall that served no purpose I could see.

Our bread-and-butter play was 35 and 36 Slant. The quarterback would sprint out and either run or pass as an option. If the fullback put the end down, the quarterback tucked the ball, ran it and picked up yardage. If the end came up and contained, 99 percent of the time the end or halfback was open in the short corner route. (contd.)

I called this play and kept the ball. The guy chasing me ran me out of bounds. I was going so fast I couldn't stop myself. I hurdled the bench and, before you knew it, hit that brick wall head on, which knocked me out. In the meantime, the guy who ran me out of bounds couldn't stop either, and he landed on my calves with his cleats. I didn't feel a thing.

Doc Knight and his trainers were hovering over me with ammonia pellets, swinging them under my nose. Well, I finally started to come to, and Doc said, "Waxie, Waxie, you okay?"

"Yeah," I said." But how are the *fans* taking it?"

Play Calling

by Bobby Franklin

My senior year, we were playing Vanderbilt in Nashville and putting a pretty good licking on them. In the third or fourth quarter, Coach Vaught took all the seniors out and sent in the sophomores. I stayed in as quarterback and knew they were tight as Dick's hat band when they got in the game. They were so nervous, they could hardly think.

I called them into the huddle. I was feeling cocky because we were winning and I was ready to have some fun. In my most serious voice, I started to call the play, a play I had just made up.

"Wing right, swing left, around the chicken coop, on two, ready, break!"

Well as soon as I clapped my hands, they broke the huddle and headed to the line of scrimmage, ready to execute.

I yelled, "Hey, come back here men. That's not even a damn play."

I had to say it twice. They were so uptight, they didn't hear me the first time.

Roast Beef Tenderloin

1 whole tenderloin, 2½ to 3 lbs.   *⅓ c. melted butter*
1 onion, thinly sliced   *salt and pepper to taste*

Preheat oven to 475 degrees. Place onion in a shallow roasting pan large enough to hold the tenderloin. Sprinkle meat generously with salt and pepper and place on top of sliced onions. Brush tops and sides with melted butter.

Roast until meat thermometer indicates desired doneness (cook the beef to just below the desired temperature because it will increase as it stands for 10 minutes before carving). Medium rare, cook 40 minutes or until meat thermometer reaches 150 to 155 degrees. Remove from oven and cover loosely with foil for 10 minutes. Carve into thin slices and serve with horseradish sauce.

Cheese Ring

1 lb. sharp cheddar cheese, grated
1 lb. medium or mild cheddar cheese, grated
1 c. mayonnaise
1 onion, grated
¼ tsp. crushed red pepper
1 c. pecans, chopped

Mix all ingredients reserving ½ cup of the pecans. Oil a bunt pan. Sprinkle the ½ cup of reserved pecans evenly in the pan and then press the cheese mixture on top and refrigerate. We like this on crackers with pepper jelly.

Bobby Franklin
Senatobia, Mississippi

Forward, Rebels

Forward Rebels, march to fame;

Hit that line and win this game.

We know that you'll fight it through

for your colors red and blue–

Rah, Rah, Rah.

Rebels, you're the Southland's pride.

Take that ball and hit your stride;

Don't stop 'til the victory's won

for your Ole Miss.

Ole Miss Fight Song

Jake Gibbs

Position & Years
Quarterback 1958-1960

Nickname
Jake

All American 1960
All SEC 1959 & 60
SEC Best Back 1960
MVP Sugar Bowl 1961
Team Co-Captain 1960

3rd in Heisman Votes 1960
College Football Hall of Fame
Miss. Sports Hall of Fame
Ole Miss Sports Hall of Fame

To Kick or Punt, That Was the Question

by Jake Gibbs

It was November 14, 1959, and Ole Miss was playing Tennessee at Crump Stadium in front of a sell-out crowd. It was 20 degrees outside and we felt the cold every down.

We were leading 7-0 going into the 2nd quarter. It was third down and we were on our own 35-yard line. I looked at Coach Vaught on the sideline. He was moving his right leg which meant he wanted us to punt.

I went to the huddle and told the guys we had to punt. Charlie Flowers, our fullback said, "Jake, let's quick kick and surprise them. I've been working on it all week."

I said, "Charlie, Coach wants us to punt."

"No, let's quick kick," he insisted.

I finally gave in and called the quick kick on the snap of two. Cowboy Woodruff was our left halfback. As the ball was snapped to Charlie, Cowboy took a couple of steps to his right. At that exact moment, Flowers kicked the ball *and* Cowboy right in the butt. It was blocked and Tennessee recovered. In just a couple of plays the score was tied 7-7. I told Charlie not to say *anything* else in the huddle.

Coach Vaught never said a word about what had happened, because we had to play defense as well as offense in those days. He didn't have a chance to chew me out.

We did score a field goal right before half and ended up winning the game 27-7.

What Coach Vaught said:

Charlie could have made a good quick kicker. Basically, the quick kick is used as an offensive weapon; it's not used as a defensive weapon. You only quick kick on first or second down. They know you're going to kick on third down. (contd.)

A quick kick is kicked a shorter distance from the line of scrimmage and it gives the other team a shorter distance to come. If Tennessee's defense had been alert, they could have blocked it. That was what worried me about calling a quick kick on third down. They know a kick has got to come.

I still ask Charlie why he ever quick kicked on third down.

Corn Squares

1 lg. onion, chopped
1 stick butter
6 eggs, beaten
1 pkg. corn muffin mix
1 can whole kernel corn, drained
1 can creamed corn
1 c. sour cream
1 c. sharp cheddar cheese, grated
1 can chopped green chilies (optional)

Preheat oven to 375 degrees. Saute onion in melted butter and set aside. Mix eggs, muffin mix and corns. Pour corn mixture into a greased 9x13 casserole dish. Top with onion mixture. Spoon sour cream over this. Grate cheese evenly over top. Bake 45 minutes. Cool and cut into squares.

Jake Gibbs
Oxford, Mississippi

The 1959 Ole Miss team, 10-1, gave up only 21 points all season. They defeated LSU in the Sugar Bowl and won the National Championship.

Larry Grantham

Position & Years
End 1957-1959

All SEC 1958 & 1959
All SEC Sophomore Team
Hula Bowl 1960
   Outstanding Lineman

Team of the Century
Miss. Sports Hall of Fame
Ole Miss Sports Hall of Fame

Stockings Off, Socks On!

by Larry Grantham

My favorite story is about the genius and superstition of Head Coach John Vaught.

After the warm-up session in preparation for the 1960 New Year's Night Sugar Bowl, the team huddled in the dressing room for final instructions. We were only minutes away from the kickoff of the rematch against our arch rival, the Tigers of LSU, thinking of nothing but avenging the loss of that terrible Halloween night game in Baton Rouge.

We had been given the option of wearing stockings that came up above our knees or just regular athletic socks that only came above our shoe tops. As the minutes ticked away, Coach Vaught gathered us around the blackboard and issued the order for all of us to take off the pro-style stockings and to put on the regular white socks.

As we hastily removed the long stockings, he hurriedly drew our Goal Line Gap Defense. He instructed us to use this defense on every down until he decided to call it off and send in a new defense.

Coach Vaught's superstition against the long stockings and his football genius put Rebel strength and defense with the Sugar Bowl. The Goal Line Gap Defense completely shut down the Tiger offense and enabled us to win 21-0. With the Gap Defense some of the Rebels didn't have any Tiger blockers assigned to them. Total domination of the defense was the result. Another bowl victory was added to the Rebel record book.

The name Ole Miss became part of the University in 1896. It was selected in a contest held to identify a new student publication, the yearbook. It was suggested by the late Miss Elma Meek of Oxford.

Fried Chicken

6 chicken breasts
1 to 1½ c. flour
1 tsp. baking powder

salt and pepper to taste
cooking oil

Rinse breasts, cover with salt and pepper and let drain. Combine flour, salt, pepper and baking soda in a brown paper bag. Shake chicken in this mixture until well coated.* Put one inch of cooking oil in a skillet. Heat to medium high. Place chicken in skillet. When breasts start sizzling, reduce heat to medium low. Cook 7 to 10 minutes on each side or until browned.

*For more flavor, refrigerate coated breasts 4 to 6 hours.

Smoked Rice

1 stick margarine
1 c. celery, chopped
1 medium onion, chopped
2 cans cream of chicken soup
1 c. chicken broth

1 tsp. Liquid Smoke
salt and pepper to taste
2 c. cooked rice
¼ tsp. garlic salt

Preheat oven to 350 degrees. Melt margarine in a heavy skillet. Add the celery and onion. Cook until onion and celery appear clear. Add soup, chicken broth, liquid smoke, and salt and pepper. Bring to a boil, then pour into a 2-quart casserole dish. Add cooked rice and garlic salt. Bake uncovered for 30 minutes.

Larry Grantham
Horn Lake, Mississippi

Individual Champions

Rushing
John "Kayo" Dottley, 1949
1,312 yards on 208 carries

Passing
Charlie Conerly, 1947
133 of 233, 7 interceptions,
1,367 yards, 18 touchdowns

Receiving
Barney Poole, 1947
52 for 513 yards, 8 touchdowns

Scoring
Parker Hall, 1938
73 points, 11 touchdowns and 7 PAT's

Interceptions
Bobby Wilson, 1949
10 for 70 yards

Pass Interception Yards
Parker Hall, 1938
128 on 7; 18.29 avg.

Punting
Frank Lambert, 1964
44.1 yards per kick; 50-2,205
Jim Miller, 1977
45.9 yards per kick, 66-3,029

Punt Returns
Junie Hovious, 1940
15.1 yards per return; 33-498

Punt-Kickoff Returns
Parker Hall, 1938
32 for 594 yards; 18.56 avg.

Kick Scoring Champions
Paige Cothern, 1955
38 on 20 PAT's, 6 field goals
Robert Khayat, 1958
34 on 22 PAT's, 4 field goals
Robert Khayat, 1959
40 on 25 PAT's, 5 field goals

All Purpose Running
Parker Hall, 1938
129.1 yards per game;
 698 Rushing
128 Interception
594 Kickoff Return

Touchdown Responsible
Parker Hall, 1938
22-11 Rush, 11 Pass

Average Gain Per Play
Parker Hall, 1936
6.46 yards

Glynn Griffing

Position & Years
Quarterback 1960-1962

All American 1962	All America Bowl 1963
All SEC 1962	College All-Star Game MVP
Team Co-Captain 1962	Atlanta Touchdown Club
Sugar Bowl MVP 1963	SEC Back of the Year 1962
Senior Bowl 1963	Ole Miss Sports Hall of Fame

Mad No More

by Glynn Griffing

My junior year at Ole Miss we were playing Mississippi State. Now Coach Vaught, whom I respect and admire to this day, had an annoying habit that drove me nuts. What he'd do is take out quarterbacks who weren't seniors and replace them with a senior every time we got within ten yards of the goal line. He was infamous for doing this.

I was having what I considered the best game of my college career. It was a super ball game. Every time we got within the 10-yard line, Coach Vaught would pull me out and put senior Doug Elmore in. I was getting really teed off, but I kept my cool the first couple of times it happened.

Finally, the third time he did it, I had the ball on about the one or two, first and goal. I looked up and here comes Doug running out on the field again. Boy, I was really hot, madder than a wet dog. Normally, I don't have a bad temper, but I had had it.

When I got to the sidelines, I was furious. Doc Knight, our trainer, asked me what was wrong and I said nothing. He prodded and finally I said, "You know what's wrong, he does it to everybody, but he's done it to me for the last time. I've had it, I'm through! I will not go back in!"

Doc patted me on the back and said, "Aw, don't worry about it."

So I went to the end of the bench and sat down on my helmet, which was against the rules. There I was trying to get Coach Vaught's attention so he could see how mad I was, and he was totally ignoring me. That made me even madder.

Right at the end of the game, we recovered a fumble down around the State goal line. About that time, Coach Vaught hollered at me to go in the game. I just sat there stunned. I couldn't believe he didn't put Elmore back in. I finally got up and ran back in.

Frank Halbert was the fullback and his brother played at State. He wanted to score a touchdown so badly it was unbelievable. I had Frank run the play and he scored. We won the game and everybody was really happy, except me.

I was still mad after the ball game. But as we were walking off the field, Coach Vaught came over, put his arm around me and said, "How would you like to be an All American and make over $100,000 next year?"

That comment absolutely blew me away. I just couldn't believe he said that, and even better, I couldn't be mad at him anymore. That was definitely a highlight I'll never forget. Coach Vaught walking me off the field, his arm around me, and he, in his infinite wisdom, knowing just what to say to me to melt away the anger. What a man!

Nixing Nitschke
by Glynn Griffing

I was fortunate to be selected to play in the All-Star game that pitted collegians against a pro team. In fact, I played in the last game the collegians ever won.

It was 1963 and we were playing the Green Bay Packers. I was the starting quarterback and, like most of my teammates, somewhat intimidated by the big, bruising pros across the line from us.

I called the first play and got under the center, looking right in the face of Ray Nitschke. He was big, mean and tough as nails. Everybody knew Ray didn't play on the football field. Just as I was about to call out signals, he growled at me, "I'm going to kick your *$%(*&@&(%!"

I was stunned. Scared to death. Speechless. I saw my life pass in front of me, but finally managed to reply, "Well, first you have to catch me."

He didn't catch me all day, and we won the game. I still think I ran faster that day than on any other during my collegiate days. You would have too, had you been running from Nitschke.

USA Today named Oxford as one of the top six college towns in the United States and called it a "thriving New South arts mecca."

Party Sandwiches by the Yard

1 18 inch-loaf of pumpernickel bread, 3½ inches in diameter
1 bunch scallions, chopped
1 8 oz. pkg. cream cheese, room temperature
3 lbs. cooked beef brisket or thinly sliced roast beef
4 tomatoes, sliced
1 lb. bacon, fried crisp
mayonnaise

Slice bread in half lengthwise, hollowing out some of the top and bottom pieces. Add chopped scallions to cream cheese and spread mixture about 1/4 inch thick on bottom half. Cover to edge of bread. Layer meat and tomato slices. Spread top half of loaf generously with the mayonnaise and put sandwich halves together. Slice sandwich diagonally at 2 inch intervals with a serrated knife.

Glynn Griffing
Jackson, Mississippi

Super Delicious Brownies

1 c. sugar
½ c. butter, melted
2 eggs
2 squares chocolate, melted
½ c. sifted flour
½ tsp. salt
1 tsp. vanilla
½ c. pecans, chopped

Preheat oven to 350 degrees. Beat sugar and butter together really well. Add the eggs and beat some more. Stir in chocolate, flour and salt. Mix until smooth. Add vanilla and nuts. Grease an 8x8x2 inch pan, pour in mixture and bake for 25 to 30 minutes. Do not over cook. Sprinkle with powdered sugar if desired.

Parker Hall

Position & Years
Halfback 1936-38

Nickname
Bullet

All American 1938
All SEC 1938
All South 1938
College All-Star Game 1939

SEC Scoring Champion 1938
Distinguished American Award
Miss. Sports Hall of Fame
Ole Miss Sports Hall of Fame

Senior Dream Season

by Parker Hall

I entered Ole Miss as a freshman in 1935. I happened to go there because one of the professors at Ole Miss had a son who was a lawyer in Tunica, and he got me in. I went out to The University of Tulsa to see about going to college there, but couldn't make any connections. I also was offered a scholarship to Southwestern, which is now Rhodes College, but I decided I'd rather go to Ole Miss because I knew some people who were already there.

When I was going to school, freshmen couldn't play varsity, but I was lucky enough to make the freshman team. I started two games my sophomore year. We weren't very good that year, and my junior year we weren't much better.

But in my senior year, we got a new head coach, Harry Mehre from Georgia. He put in the Notre Dame Box, an offense that fit me to a tee. I liked it and Coach Mehre too.

We went to LSU for our season opener. I got lucky and ran a punt back 65 yards to the 1-yard line. We beat LSU 20-7. I had the best time that day. The whole team did. It was true then and it's true now, there is no substitute for winning.

This was the first time Ole Miss had beaten LSU in ten years. Even better, it was the beginning of a winning season for the Rebels. We finished 9-2 in 1938, losing only to Tennessee and Vanderbilt. I had the time of my life playing football for Ole Miss and Coach Mehre.

Four Ole Miss players have scored in the top five in Heisman Votes; Charlie Conerly 4th (1947), Charlie Flowers 5th (1959), Jake Gibbs 3rd (1960) and Archie Manning 4th (1969) and 3rd (1970).

Sour Cream Cole Slaw

1 c. sour cream
3 T. lemon juice
1 tsp. salt
1 tsp. green onion, chopped

1 tsp. celery seed
dash pepper
1 tsp. sugar
4 c. raw cabbage, shredded

Combine all ingredients and pour over cabbage. Toss well and refrigerate.

Tita's Salsa

1 sm. can chili peppers, drained
Newman's Own Olive Oil and Vinegar Dressing
green and black olives to taste, chopped
2-4 green onions, with tops, chopped
3-5 tomatoes

Mix above with dressing. Chill and serve. This is wonderful for tailgating. Bring plenty of chips.

Parker Hall
Vicksburg, Mississippi

Tomato Sandwiches

4 loaves bread
8 medium tomatoes

salt and pepper to taste
mayonnaise

Cut bread into rounds. Slice tomatoes thinly. Add salt and pepper and let stand one hour. Spread mayonnaise on bread rounds. Place tomato slices on 1/2 the rounds. Top with other bread round.

To store until serving time, put wax paper between each layer, cover with damp towels and refrigerate.

Tailgating hint: Take sandwiches dry. Put out the platter of sandwiches with mayonnaise on the side.

Football Snackers

1 10 oz. pkg. oyster crackers
1 pkg. Hidden Valley Ranch salad dressing
³/₄ c. vegetable oil
½ tsp. garlic powder
½ tsp. dill weed
½ tsp. lemon pepper

Mix all ingredients. Let sit until crackers absorb all of the oil.
Store in airtight containers. Great for tailgating.

Crunchy Pecan Cookies

½ c. shortening   *¼ tsp. salt*
1 box powdered sugar   *½ tsp. soda*
1 stick butter   *1 tsp. vanilla*
2 eggs, beaten very well   *1 c. pecans, finely chopped*
2½ c. flour

Preheat oven to 350 degrees. Cream shortening and butter thoroughly. Gradually add sugar and cream. Add eggs. Sift the flour, soda and salt together. Reduce mixer to low and add flour mixture. Add vanilla. Stir in pecans. Drop by tip of a teaspoon onto greased cookie sheet, two inches apart. Top with pecan halves. Bake for about 10 minutes.

Harry Harrison

Position & Years
Safety 1971-73

Nickname
Horse

All American 1973
All SEC 1973
Academic All SEC 1972

SEC Interception Champ 1972
Ole Miss Sports Hall of Fame

Imperfect Timing

by Harry Harrison

We went to Tiger Stadium November 4, 1972, to win the ball game. And we did–for 59 minutes and 59 seconds. Although the record book says LSU won 17-16, in my mind, that is dead wrong. Let me explain.

The minute we walked on the field to warm up, the LSU student section, packed already, started throwing oranges at us, an indication of their intention to win the game and go to the Orange Bowl. We had a different idea and absolutely killed them the entire game. We had them beat all over the field.

We were leading 16-10 very late in the game. With about three minutes to go, we kicked a field goal. The ref signaled no good, but it was a controversial call. We thought it went through. That's when LSU got the ball back and started marching toward our goal line.

With four seconds left in the game, they drove to our 11-yard line and called time-out. They came back on the field and ran a fake draw play. Quarterback Bert Jones took the snap, back pedaled, faked a draw, and threw it over the middle. The pass was incomplete, knocked down by Mickey Fratesi. We were already celebrating our victory, but when we looked up at the scoreboard, there was still one second left on the clock.

With one second to go, they ran the pick play, which was illegal then. In a pick play, the receivers aren't running routes, they're just picking off a linebacker so the quarterback can throw to the underneath guy.

I was covering the receiver on the inside: Fratesi was covering the outside receiver; and Bobby Bailess was the lineman who got picked off trying to cover running back Brad Davis. I left my guy to cover Davis. Jones admitted after the game, and I agree, that his pass to Davis was probably the worst he had ever thrown in his life.

When I got to Davis, he was standing right at the corner of the pile-on and the out of bounds. He never really had control of the ball. He was juggling it when I got there and I pushed him. Unfortunately, the ref was only looking to see if he stepped across the line. He did step across, but he never had control of the ball.

So with no time left on the clock, LSU supposedly scored a touchdown, which tied the game. And, with no time on the clock, they kicked the extra point and ended up winning by one point. They didn't beat us, they only won the game.

For a long time after that game, when you crossed the bridge at Vicksburg to go into Louisiana there were signs that read, "Now Entering Louisiana, Set Your Clock Back Four Seconds."

I'd like to talk to timekeeper Jim Campbell about what happened to the clock that night in Tiger Stadium. It still haunts me. And I can assure you of one thing: It didn't matter if you were wearing a Rolex or a Timex at that game, time stood still for four seconds.

Quick Quiche

2 lbs. cheddar cheese, grated
4 oz. jar sliced mushrooms, drained
4 oz. jar green olives, sliced, reserve juice
1 dozen eggs, beaten
salt and pepper to taste

Preheat oven to 350 degrees. In a 9x13 casserole dish layer 1 lb. of the cheese. Cover with mushrooms, olives and remaining cheese. Mix the olive juice with the beaten eggs, salt and pepper. Pour over cheese mixture. Sprinkle with paprika and bake 30 to 40 minutes. Cut into squares. May be made ahead of time.

Harry Harrison
Jackson, Mississippi

Tailgating necessities: Napkins, paper plates, eating utensils, garbage bags, cups, paper towels, towelettes, table cloth, chairs and plenty of ice.

Broccoli Salad

2 bunches fresh broccoli
¼ c. stuffed olives, sliced
1 sm. bunch green onions, with tops, chopped
½ c. Parmesan cheese
½ c. zesty Italian dressing
½ to ¾ c. mayonnaise
bacon bits (optional)
hard boiled eggs, finely diced (optional)

Cut buds off broccoli and set aside. Peel the stalks off the broccoli and cook in a small amount of salted water for 10 minutes. Drain and cool. Toss chilled broccoli, olives, onions, and cheese. Add dressing and toss. Add enough mayonnaise to hold ingredients together. Garnish with eggs and bacon bits, if desired.

Pink Lady Cake

Cake

1 box white cake mix
1 c. vegetable oil
1 box strawberry gelatin
⅔ c. water
4 eggs

Preheat oven to 350 degrees. Put cake mix, oil, gelatin and water in a mixing bowl. Add eggs one at a time, beating after each. Pour into two greased round cake pans. Bake until done.

Icing

1 stick oleo, softened
1 box powdered sugar
½ c. frozen strawberries, thawed

Gradually add powdered sugar to softened oleo. Mix in strawberries, a few at a time. Be careful not to add too many strawberries, it may not take the full ½ cup. Blend and spread on cake.

Stan Hindman

Position & Years
Guard 1963-65

Nickname
Haystack

All American 1965
All SEC 1963, 64 & 65
Team Co-Captain 1965
Sophomore All SEC 1963
Academic All American

College All-Star Game 1966
Ole Miss Hall of Fame
Team of the Century
Miss. Sports Hall of Fame
Ole Miss Sports Hall of Fame

Sea Cruise

by Stan Hindman

Ray Beddingfield, Tommy Murphy and I spent the summer of 1963 working for Ryder Truck Lines in Tampa, Florida. The Athletic Department at Ole Miss would find jobs for football players that were extremely physical so we'd keep in shape throughout the summer. I guess it worked because we lifted weights during the day and loaded trucks from five in the afternoon until one in the morning.

One calm, beautiful afternoon we decided to go sailing. As we were on a limited budget, we rented a very small boat–so small in fact, that it looked like it came out of a cereal box. We got the boat to the water line, loaded up and started out into Tampa Bay.

It was kind of dull out there at first. There was hardly any wind. We were just sitting out there in the hot sun. Finally, the wind started to pick up and Ray, at the helm, got really excited. I was at the stern, and as the wind continued to pick up and the sail grew full, we were hitting the waves and really making headway. Ray was having a ball.

It didn't take long for the weather to worsen, and we started getting a little concerned. It got very dark and a big storm rolled in. By now we were just plain scared and wanted to get back to shore, so we were working hard to reach any land we could find.

All of a sudden, we got hit by lightening. It just cracked. I guess it hit the mast. I thought I was dead. I didn't feel anything at first and then I started tingling all over. I turned to Tommy, who was in the middle seat and told him I'd been struck. He just stared at me with a stunned look on his face and didn't say a word. He shook his head as if to say he'd been hit too. We both turned back to look at Ray. He had his hands on the sides of the boat, and was starring straight ahead. It was like he was in a catatonic state.

When we came to our senses, we started paddling like crazy for the nearest land. We ended up getting into MacDill Air Force Base, across the bay from where we embarked. We pulled the boat up on shore and promptly were picked up by the military police.

We were arrested and taken to the brig. It took awhile for us to talk our way out of there. (contd.)

This event really changed Ray. He was absolutely possessed by the whole experience. Some guy on the truck dock told him that sometimes when you were hit by lightening, you'd be fine and then drop dead the next week. Well that's all he thought about.

Later in the summer, we went to see *Lawrence of Arabia*. The whole personality of Lawrence of Arabia captivated Ray, and he began to read all he could about him. He then began to take on a lot of his traits.

We returned to Ole Miss to start the fall semester, and for most of that year, Ray was influenced by our experience at sea and his interest in Lawrence of Arabia. Burning candles and sitting in the middle of the room were just part of his regimen.

The whole summer was a good experience. We all learned a lot, and Ray had a life-altering experience that made him stronger.

Graham Cracker Cookies

24 graham crackers
1 stick butter
1 c. light brown sugar, packed firmly
1 c. pecans, chopped

Preheat oven to 350 degrees. Put crackers on ungreased 10x12 cookie sheet. Melt butter and sugar in saucepan. When done, stir constantly for exactly two minutes. Remove and add pecans. Spread evenly over the crackers. Bake 10-12 minutes. When warm, remove from pan and cut crackers in half.

Ole Miss Bowl Record

Year	Bowl	Opponent	Score
1936	Orange	Catholic U.	19-20
1948	Delta	TCU	13-9
1953	Sugar	Georgia Tech	7-24
1955	Sugar	Navy	0-21
1956	Cotton	TCU	14-13
1958	Sugar	Texas	39-7
1958	Gator	Florida	7-3
1960	Sugar	LSU	21-0
1961	Sugar	Rice	14-6
1962	Cotton	Texas	7-12
1963	Sugar	Arkansas	17-13
1964	Sugar	Alabama	7-12
1964	Bluebonnet	Tulsa	7-14
1965	Liberty	Auburn	13-7
1966	Bluebonnet	Texas	0-19
1967	Sun	UT-El Paso	7-14
1968	Liberty	Virginia Tech	34-17
1970	Sugar	Arkansas	27-22
1971	Gator	Auburn	28-35
1971	Peach	Georgia Tech	41-18
1983	Independence	Air Force	3-9
1986	Independence	Texas Tech	20-17
1989	Liberty	Air Force	42-29
1991	Gator	Michigan	3-35
1992	Liberty	Air Force	13-0

Won: 14 Lost: 11

Robert Khayat

Position & Years
Place-kicker & Guard 1957-59

Academic All America 1959	Kick Scoring Champion 1959
Academic All SEC 1959	Distinguished American Award
College All-Star Game 1960	Team of the Century
Kick Scoring Champion 1958	Ole Miss Sports Hall of Fame

Smoke Screen

by Robert Khayat

In a team meeting, Coach Bruiser Kinard told us he had heard that some of us had been smoking.

He turned to Richard "Possum" Price and said, "How about it, Possum?"

Richard, one of the finest and most honest people who ever lived, replied, "Coach, I won't lie, I smoke."

Coach said, "Possum, you can't smoke and play for Ole Miss!"

"Coach you don't understand, I've smoked since I was seven years old. I have to have a cigarette after supper."

Coach Kinard thought a minute, and realizing that Richard was one of the best lineman on the team responded, "Well then Possum, just cut down on the number of cigarettes that you do smoke."

Robert Khayat is a true example of one who graduated from The University but never left Ole Miss. Following his outstanding college career, both athletically and academically, he left Mississippi to play professional football for the Washington Redskins.

Following his professional football career, Khayat returned to Ole Miss and attended law school. Graduating third in the 1966 School of Law class, he began teaching in the law school on the Ole Miss campus in 1969. After both teaching and practicing law, Khayat attended Yale University on the Sterling Fellowship during the 1980-81 academic year. At Yale, he earned his Master's Degree. Khayat returned to Ole Miss in 1981 and resumed his position as law professor.

Khayat was named chancellor of The University of Mississippi July 1, 1995.

Going Bananas Sandwich

banana
peanut butter
light bread

Whip peanut butter and a banana into a smooth cream and spread on light bread.

Robert Khayat
Oxford, Mississippi

Editor's Note: If the Chancellor of Ole Miss were tailgating with me, here's what I would serve him.

Momma's Fried Kibbi

2 lbs. heavy round steak, all fat removed and ground twice
4 medium onions
1 c. #2 wheat (bulghur)
salt and pepper
oil for frying

Wash the wheat and then soak it in cold water for 15 minutes. Drain all the water off, making sure the wheat is as dry as possible. Put the onions in the food processor and pulse until they are pulverized. Put meat, onions, wheat, salt and pepper in a large bowl. Use your hands to mix well. Shape into patties and fry until dark brown. Make a day ahead of time and put in the refrigerator until you pack it in your ice chest for the Grove. Delicious served hot or cold.

Fudge Muffins

2 sticks margarine
6 T. cocoa
1³/₄ c. sugar
¹/₈ tsp. salt

1 c. flour
4 eggs
1 tsp. vanilla
2 c. pecans, finely chopped

Preheat oven to 325 degrees. Melt butter. Stir in cocoa, add sugar, salt and flour. Beat well with a spoon. Stir in eggs, one at a time. Add vanilla and pecans. Place in miniature muffin tins that have been sprayed with cooking spray. Fill 3/4 full and bake 15 to 20 minutes.

Coconut Pie

This pie makes its own crust.

4 eggs
1³/₄ c. sugar
¹/₂ c. flour
2 c. milk

¹/₄ c. melted butter
1¹/₂ c. coconut
1 tsp. vanilla

Preheat oven to 350 degrees. Combine all ingredients in order given. Pour into a greased pie pan. Bake 30 to 45 minutes or until golden brown.

Onion Dip

1 c. mayonnaise
1 8 oz. pkg. cream cheese
1 package onion dip mix

3 or 4 green onion tops, diced
4 or 5 slices bacon, fried crisp

Mix together, chill and serve with your favorite chips. Better if prepared ahead of time.

Jimmy Lear

Position & Years	**Nickname**
Quarterback 1950-52	"King" Lear

All American 1952	Colonel Rebel
All SEC 1951 & 52	Ole Miss Hall of Fame
MVP 1952 & 53	Miss. Sports Hall of Fame
SEC Back of the Week 1952	Ole Miss Sports Hall of Fame

Riding Shoulder High

by Jimmy Lear

November 15, 1952, was one of the most gorgeous days I ever remember seeing in Oxford, Mississippi. It could not have been a more perfect day to play a football game, especially one as important as this game against Maryland. Ole Miss had never played Maryland, but for some reason, Tennessee was dropped from the schedule that year, so we put Maryland in that slot.

I remember the game vividly. Coach Vaught spent a tremendous amount of time telling us about the significance of beating Maryland. They had won 32 consecutive games and were ranked number one in the country. It looked like they were going to be national champs again, but being a determined bunch, we were devising an aggressive plan to put an end to their domination.

I was a senior playing quarterback and I loved our offense, the Split T. We had only been running it a couple of years, but it suited me well. It required the quarterback to do a lot of running and option play off the defensive ends. Back then, we didn't pass very much, but that beautiful November day, when I did pass, our receivers were catching everything that I threw to them.

Maryland ran the same offense we did, but that day we ran it better. I can still see Ray Howell catching a pass for a touchdown early in the game, Bud Slay catching a pass at about the 2-yard line late in the game when the score was tied and my roommate, Wilson (Wizzy) Dillard, scoring the winning touchdown.

But what still flabbergasts me is what happened when the game was over and we had won. The whole student body came out on the field and started lifting us up on their shoulders. We had no idea that was going to happen; we had never experienced anything like that, and it overwhelmed us. It was an experience I'll treasure for years to come.

What Coach Vaught said:

Jimmy Lear played an outstanding ball game that day. Our quarterbacks called their own plays. We taught them the game plan, gave them the plan completely, and were there to guide and direct, but they called the shots in the huddle. That day, against Maryland, Jimmy Lear called a perfect ball game.

Pecan, Bell Pepper & Black Olive Sandwich

pecans, chopped
bell pepper,chopped
black olives, chopped

mayonnaise
your favorite bread

Combine equal amounts of chopped pecans, chopped bell pepper, and chopped black olives. Mix with enough mayonnaise to hold together. Spread on your favorite bread.

Tuna in Pita Bread with Bean Sprouts

1 can white tuna, drained
juice of a lemon
Chopped bell pepper, celery and spring onions to taste

Mix above with mayonnaise. Fill a pita pocket 2/3 full. Top with chopped Spanish olives, chopped tomato and bean sprouts.

Jimmy Lear
Indianola, Mississippi

A Conversation with John Vaught

You were line coach at Ole Miss in 1946, and the team had a losing season. The following year Red Drew left for Alabama and you were named head coach. To what do you attribute that appointment?

J.V. *Red Drew sent me to scout the Arkansas/University of Texas ball game. I got a good scouting report. I told Coach Drew we could beat Arkansas. He told me to put the defense and offense on the board. We beat Arkansas 9-7, one of two games we won that year. When the press asked Drew about the turnover in the program, he said, "You've got to give credit to John Vaught. He set up the offense and defense, everybody did their job and we did it." I think that's the reason I was asked to take over his job when he left.*

Did you jump at the chance to take the job?

J.V. *No. I didn't want the job.*

Why not?

J.V. *For one simple reason; recruiting. We could recruit no one, especially coming off a 2-7 season. I told the administration I could not take a job if I couldn't recruit. I knew I couldn't win without recruiting, and I wanted to recruit in Mississippi. We had very few Mississippi boys on the 1946 team.*

What changed your mind?

J.V. *I got with five or six alumni from around the state. They promised if I took the job, they would do everything they could to help me recruit and influence Mississippi players in their area to come to Ole Miss. I took the job, and alumni from across the state were a tremendous help.*

Recruiting was and is the definite key to perpetual winning. Why do you think it has become increasingly difficult to recruit?

J.V. *Most college prospects today want to go to bigger schools that get a lot of publicity. They think it helps them get bigger pro contracts.*

119

You coached Archie Manning. Was he an easy recruit for Ole Miss?

J.V. Archie came from Drew. He played football, but there were only about 15 players on his team. You can't expect a team that small to do too much on the field, but they did well in their confer- ence. He didn't have a big football reputation. In fact, not too many people knew about him. We really recruited him as an ath- lete, not a football player. We saw him play basketball and knew he was a good, good athlete.

What did you look for in recruits?

J.V. We didn't necessarily care what position they played. We recruited athletes. Back then, most high school coaches around the state were placing their best players at either fullback or quarter- back. Most of the time, those were the two best athletes on the team. We were signing ten or twelve fullbacks and quarterbacks a season. We'd pick the players with the best ability for those posi- tions. We placed our other players in whatever positions they qual- ified for. The best team I can remember had a line made up of seven former fullbacks.

What teams did you want to beat most badly?

J.V. Well, you want to beat them all. Of course, I wanted to beat State, because they're the local competition. I think our contracts depended on the outcome of that game. And LSU and Tennessee. Ole Miss had never beaten Tennessee until I became head coach.

That must have been a thrill.

J.V. You bet. We played in Memphis in 1947 and beat them 43-13. Red Drew, my former boss, sent me a telegram after that game; "Congratulations. The best football game since the invention of the forward pass." Getting that wire meant the world to me.

Did you have any pre-game rituals, good luck charms or superstitions when you coached.?

J.V. I didn't have any rituals. I was not superstitious. I didn't have any good luck charms. I just believed in hard work, commitment from the athletes and help from God.

Brian Lee

Position & Years
Kicker 1989-92

Academic All American Dist. 6   All-Time Leading Scorer

Academic All SEC   Most Field Goals in One Game

SEC Player of the Week 1991

Picture-perfect Kick

by Brian Lee

I made my last-ever kick in Vaught-Hemingway Stadium with about half an inch to spare. This kick put me into first place in career scoring. I owe a world of thanks to Rogers Stephens, who not only held the ball, but had his father perfectly positioned to take a picture of me and the kick. The photo below is one of my most cherished possessions.

Back on the field, David Vinson, my roommate, wrestled the ball away from an equipment manager so I could hand it to my dad in the stands.

Later that same quarter, we held Mississippi State for 11 plays inside our 10-yard line. Students flooded the field, the goal posts came down and Coach Jackie Sherrill, had to swallow his "Ole Miss will never beat us" promise. What better day to be a Rebel?

Brian Lee (number 8) watches as his record-setting kick goes through the uprights at Vaught-Hemingway Stadium. Ole Miss beat State 17-10, November 28, 1992.

Dog's Dog

by Brian Lee

I can't remember a practice at Ole Miss without thinking about GB, Coach Billy Brewer's golden lab. Always a fixture, he followed at Coach's heels. This made live field-goal practice an adventure from time to time.

Coach Brewer was in charge of the kickers and usually stood within a few steps of us. Of course, you could count on GB to be right there, wandering in and out of the line of scrimmage or between the ball and me. He nearly blocked several of my kicks in his days as the official dog of Rebel football.

Rebel Red Salsa

2 tomatoes sliced and chopped
1 sm. can tomato sauce
1 sm. can chopped green chilies
1 sm. can chopped black olives
1 bunch green onions, chopped (use all parts)
garlic and salt to taste
3 T. red wine vinegar
2 T. cooking oil

Mix all together and let marinate in refrigerator overnight. The longer it sits, the better it gets. Serve with your favorite corn chips. Keep in the ice chest on the way to the Grove.

I've enjoyed this with the Walsh and Brown families of Forrest, MS for years. I thank them for supplying me the recipe—B.L.

Brian Lee
Atlanta, Georgia

Kris Mangum

Position & Years
Tight End 1994-96

All American 1996   All SEC 1995 & 96
All American Hon. Men. 1995

Freshmen on Parade

by Kris Mangum

Freshmen football players arrive on campus about a week before the varsity team checks in. This gives them an opportunity to get adjusted, start learning the playing system and get to know the coaches.

Once the upperclassmen come in, serious practice starts, including two-a-days, when we practice twice a day. Traditionally, the night before these rigorous workouts begin, freshmen get their heads shaved. We set up our makeshift "barber shop" in the hall of Kinard and bring our customers in for the ceremonial balding.

In my senior year, after we had finished our handiwork, we decided to have the freshman put on a talent show for us. We set up chairs downstairs and each guy or group of guys performed. We all laughed so hard. Watching big, burly he-men singing, dancing and entertaining a bunch of unruly Rebels was absolutely hysterical.

It then occurred to us that sorority rush was going on and hundreds of girls were participating. We knew we had to take advantage of that situation, so we got on the phone and told our friends who lived over there to go outside, a parade was about to begin.

We told the guys to strip down to their shorts and then loaded them in pickup trucks and headed to the Grove, right at the top of Sorority Row. At that point we told the freshmen to get out, run down the street and get back to the dorm as best they could.

You should have seen it. Bald freshmen football players, with nothing on but their shorts, running down Sorority Row with upperclassmen following them in trucks and cars, blowing horns and whooping and hollering. But the greatest part was the hundreds of girls lined up on both sides of the street. As the guys ran through them, they started yelling "Hotty Totty" and screaming "Go Rebels"!

The guys loved it. They were running along with their fists in the air, waving at the girls and having the time of their lives. Running down Sorority Row at Ole Miss, being the center of attention with hundreds of girls watching is every guy's dream. They were living it. (contd.)

Unfortunately, with all the commotion, campus police arrived just in time to catch the varsity players. We thought we had really done something, but we were the ones who got caught *and* in trouble.

Hanky Panky

1 lb. hamburger	*½ tsp. oregano*
1 lb. sausage	*½ tsp. garlic powder*
1 lb. processed cheese	*English muffins*

Brown hamburger and sausage. Drain. Add cheese, oregano and garlic powder. Serve over English Muffins.

Mom takes a grill and heats this up after the game—K.M.

Pecan Tassies

3 oz. cream cheese, softened	*1 c. flour*
1 stick oleo, softened	

Mix above, make a ball and refrigerate 2 to 3 hours. Then pinch off small balls of mixture and press in miniature muffin tins.

Filling

1 c. brown sugar	1 egg
2 T. oleo	¾ c. pecans, chopped
2 tsp. vanilla	

Preheat oven to 350 degrees. Mix filling ingredients together real well. Spoon into muffin tins over crust mixture. Bake until brown, about 15 or 20 minutes.

Kris Mangum
Charlotte, North Carolina

126

Apple Pecan Cake

1½ c. oil
2 c. sugar
2 eggs
3 c. flour
4 lg. apples, diced

1½ tsp. soda
½ tsp. salt
1 tsp. vanilla
1 tsp. cinnamon
1 c. pecans

Preheat oven to 300 degrees. Mix and cream all ingredients. Pour into a greased tube pan. Bake one hour or until done when tested.

Nibblers

1 6 oz. pkg. pretzels
1 lb. salted peanuts
1 box Rice Chex cereal
1 box Cheerios
½ c. Worcestershire sauce

2 T. garlic salt
2 T. onion salt
1 T. celery salt
2 sticks margarine

Preheat oven to 225 degrees. Melt oleo with sauce and salts. Pour over cereal mix. Mix thoroughly. Bake in a large flat pan for one hour, stirring occasionally.

Caramel Corn

½ c. light corn syrup
1 c. butter
1 tsp. salt

2 c. dark brown sugar
1 tsp. soda
7½ quarts popcorn, popped

Preheat oven to 200 degrees. Bring syrup, butter, salt and brown sugar to a rolling boil. Remove from heat and add soda, beat well. Gradually pour over popcorn, stirring until completely coated. Bake for one hour, stirring every 15 minutes. Remove, cool and store in airtight containers.

Archie Manning

Position & Years
Quarterback 1968-70

All American 1969 & 70	SEC Player of Year, Offense
All SEC 1969 & 70	Miss. Sportsman of the Year
All South 1970	Team of the Century
Team Co-Captain 1970	Ole Miss Sports Hall of Fame
Outstanding Back in America	Miss. Sports Hall of Fame

Sophomore Starter

by Archie Manning

In the Memphis State*-Ole Miss football series, 1967 is a historic year. They beat us for the first time ever. I was a freshman, sitting in the stands with my classmates, heads shaved, beanies on and yelling for victory. It wasn't to be. The next week the varsity team was not in the best of spirits and they took it out on us.

The following year, we were determined MSU wasn't going to start a winning streak. The press had been writing about the game all summer, and there was quite a bit of hoopla about what would happen opening game. There was a lot of discussion about how many sophomores would be playing, and also that I was starting as quarterback. They tell me I was the first sophomore quarterback ever to start for Coach Vaught. Talk about pressure.

We got ready to go up there and play, and I was scared to death. Growing up in Drew, Mississippi, probably the biggest crowd I had ever played in front of was 1,200 people. Now, all of a sudden, I was playing a college football game in front of 50,000 screaming fans, about half of them for the Rebels and half for the Tigers.

One of my best friends was Skipper Jernigan, who played left guard. Skipper was still 18-years old, and he was starting in the offensive line. Before the game, he and I were sitting in the dressing room scared to death, looking through the program.

It was there we discovered that Memphis State had an outstanding linebacker, Joe Rushing. Joe had graduated high school, gone to college for a while, left for a stint in the military, and was now back with the Tigers. He was 26-years old.

So here was 18-year-old Skipper with no college game experience up against 26-year-old Joe, full of experience and with a face only a mother could love. Well, we never should have seen that. It made Skipper a little nervous. But it made me real nervous because Skipper was going to be blocking him, or at least giving it a try. (contd.)

*Now called The University of Memphis.

We went out and played like we were scared in the first half. I think we had one first down. Coach Vaught gave us a little talk at the half. Finally, we got over the crowd, the noise, and the jitters and managed to beat Memphis State 21-7.

During my college career I played in bigger stadiums with larger, nosier crowds, but I don't think I ever played in one that seemed as big as that jammed house in Memphis on my first Ole Miss game, September 21, 1968, at Liberty Bowl Stadium.

Lace Cookies

2 c. old-fashioned rolled oats
1 T. flour
2 c. white sugar
½ tsp. salt

2 sticks butter, melted
2 eggs, beaten
1 tsp. vanilla

Preheat oven to 325 degrees. Put the oats, flour, sugar and salt into a large bowl and mix well. Pour very hot butter over the mixture and stir until the sugar has melted. Add eggs and vanilla, stir well. Cover cookie sheets with ungreased aluminum foil. Drop 1/2 level teaspoons of the mixture on foil, two inches apart. Cook 10 to 12 minutes. Watch carefully. When cookies are completely cooled, foil will peel off. Store in airtight containers. Makes about 6 dozen.

A favorite with the Manning boys, especially for tailgate picnics–Olivia Manning

Archie Manning
New Orleans, Louisiana

Team Pleasing Tarts

2 8 oz. pkgs. cream cheese
¾ c. sugar
3 eggs, separated
4 T. butter, melted
1 c. graham crackers, rolled finely

Filling

1 pint sour cream   2 tsp. vanilla
5 T. sugar

Preheat oven to 325 degrees. Blend cream cheese and sugar with mixer on medium speed. Beat egg yolks and add to mixture. Beat whites until stiff and fold gently into sugar mixture, using a wooden spoon. Grease tart muffin tins with butter. Fill each tin with graham cracker crumbs. Turn over on wax paper to remove excess crumbs. Fill muffin tin with one teaspoon of the cream cheese mixture. Bake for 15 minutes. Cool tins on wire rack until mixture sinks in middle. Add ½ teaspoon sour cream filling in center of crust. Return to oven and bake five minutes at 350 degrees, then let stand for 15 minutes. Remove. Place on wire racks to cool completely. Top each tart with your favorite fruit pie filling.

Winning Walnuts

6 c. water   ½ c. sugar
16 oz. walnuts   salt
vegetable oil

Boil water in a four-quart saucepan. Add walnuts and boil one minute. Drain. Rinse in hot water. Put in a bowl and add sugar. Stir until sugar dissolves. In a saucepan at medium to high heat, heat one inch of salad oil. Put in half of the nuts. Stir constantly for five minutes, using a slotted spoon. Drain in colander. Lightly salt. Lay on wax paper. Repeat with remaining half. Store in airtight container.

131

Crawford Mims

Position & Years
Guard 1950-53

Consensus All American 1953
All SEC 1952 & 53
All South 1953
Jacobs Best Blocker Award
North South Shrine Bowl MVP

College All-Star Game 1954
Athlon Sports All Time Rebel
    Team
Miss. Sports Hall of Fame
Ole Miss Sports Hall of Fame

Les is More

by Crawford Mims

The greatest thing that ever happened to me was going to Ole Miss to play football. I had a great time, made lifelong friends and won many accolades during my years there.

Because the Korean War was going on during my tenure, we had fewer players and had to learn to play both offense and defense. It was easy for some of us and hard for others, but we did the best we could and I did play on both sides of the ball.

The years went by in a whirl, and I had decided that I thought I was pretty good. Coach Vaught talked to me about playing pro ball and told me I was too small. I didn't want to believe him.

I had been to the North-South Shrine Game in Miami and was fortunate enough to be named Most Valuable Player as a lineman. I also had played in the Senior Bowl and was invited to play in the All-Star Game in Chicago. The College All Stars played against a pro team, the Detroit Lions.

We were practicing at Purdue University under the leadership of Jim Tatum, head coach at Maryland. Coach Tatum decided that we could beat the pros if we made them play both sides of the ball. He figured the pros had been playing one way for so long they couldn't go back to playing two ways again.

Game day came. We had 53 guys from all over the country, most of them All Americans, All Conference, All Everything and we were convinced we could win the game.

We kicked off to them, thinking we were going to win. I started as defensive guard playing head-on against a guy named Les Bingham. He weighed about 390 pounds on a light day. I got down on all fours and realized I couldn't see over, under or around him.

The first play I hit him real hard and that didn't do anything. It was kind of like a gnat flying up against a mule. He just reached out and pulled me down. After about two or three of these plays, I went to the ref.

"That guy is holding me," I said.

"Look, son, don't tell me your problems, you're playing real football now. You're out of the peewee league."

So I backed up four or five steps where I thought I could at least

133

see or feel or do something back there. I realized they were going to throw a swing pass, which I almost intercepted. But, about that time Coach Tatum took me out of the game.

"What in the world are you doing out there?" he asked.

"Coach, if you knew how tough it was out there in the middle of that line, then you'd know what I was doing. I was trying to get away from that guy! I can't do anything out there. I can't see nothing, I can't hear nothing, I can't do nothing."

We lost 28-0. I ended up in the hospital, still dreaming of playing for the New York Giants, who had drafted me. But the longer I lay there, the more sense I got. I picked up the phone.

"Coach Vaught, I've decided you were right, I'm too small to play in the pros," I confessed.

He agreed, and told me to come back to Ole Miss, finish my degree and coach with him, which I did. At the end of that year, he offered me a full-time coaching job, making $5,500 a year. I thought I would take it because I liked coaching, I liked Coach Vaught and I thought $5,500 was a lot of money.

I talked it over with my father-in-law, who told me I could do better working for him in Vicksburg. So I loaded up and went to work for him in the grocery business making $100 a week. My wife, Boop, and I were living with my in-laws and had no expenses. Man, I thought I had hit pay dirt.

After our third child was born, my father-in-law said to me, "Son, either you have to go or I have to go, but one of us is moving out."

Boop and I bought a house, had two more kids and I opened the first convenience store in Mississippi.

Life's been good to me, and I have Les Bingham to thank for making a believer out of me.

Fancy Tuna Salad

2 - 6½ oz. cans tuna, drained and flaked
3 T. mayonnaise
4 green onions with tops, chopped
4 boiled eggs, chopped
1 apple, cored, coarsely chopped or grated
½ c. sweet pickle relish
½ c. chopped celery
1 tsp. lemon pepper
1 tsp. mustard
dash of dried dill weed
½ c. chopped pecans
green grapes, sliced (optional)
½ c. green olives, sliced (optional)

Combine all ingredients and stir until smooth. Take tailgating in an ice chest.

Peppy Pimento Cheese

1 8 oz. pkg. cream cheese
1 c. mayonnaise
1 c. Swiss cheese, shredded
1 c. American cheese, shredded
1 sm. jar chopped pimento
1 tsp. Worcestershire sauce
½ tsp. onion powder
¼ tsp. hot sauce
1½ tsp. grated Parmesan cheese
½ tsp. seasoned salt
1 c. pecans, chopped

Soften cream cheese and combine with mayonnaise; blend until smooth. Add the Swiss and American cheese; beat well. Add pimento, Worcestershire, onion powder and hot sauce; beat well. Sprinkle with Parmesan cheese, seasoned salt and pecans. Serve as a spread for sandwiches or with your favorite crackers. Refrigerate until serving time.

Crawford Mims
Vicksburg, Mississippi

135

Chris Mitchell

Position & Years
Cornerback & Safety 1987-90

Nickname
Creek

All American Hon. Mention
All SEC 1991
Sports Illustrated Player of
    the Week 1990
Gillette Player of the Week

Chucky Mullins Courage
Award
    First Recipient
Senior Bowl 1991
Team of the Century

The Big Hit

by Chris Mitchell

In 1990, Ole Miss played Arkansas in Little Rock. The Razorbacks had joined the SEC in August of that year, and both of our teams were out to prove something: Ole Miss, that we had experience in the SEC and could beat a rookie team, and Arkansas, that they could compete in a conference other than the Southwest. The stadium echoed, "Wooo, Pig! Sooie!" forever and the game was turning into a fight until the finish.

At the very end of the game, we were winning 21-17 and they were threatening to score. We were determined to hold them and win the game. They got to the goal line and it was do–or–die for both teams.

It was the last play of the game and they were about to score. They gave the ball to Ron Dickerson. As he headed to the end zone, I hit him head on at the six-inch line to keep him from scoring the touchdown that would have beaten us.

As the buzzer sounded that the game was over, I fell to the ground. I had jammed my neck so hard during that big hit, I could barely move. My buddy, Chauncey Godwin, was grabbing my jersey, yelling that we had won. As excited as I was, all I could think was, "Don't even touch me man. Let go of me. My neck is killing me."

I looked out of the corner of my eye and saw our head trainer, Leroy Mullins coming toward me. Get up, I told myself, because if he catches you down, it's therapy tomorrow, and I hated therapy. All of us did. Therapy was three times a day and hard work. I mustered all the energy I could, got up and started trotting toward the dressing room. I was on one side of the field and "Dr. Le" was on the other.

"Creek, you okay?" he hollered from the other side.

"I'm fine Dr. Le, just fine," I lied.

So we get in the dressing room and he said, "Creek, turn around and look at me." (contd.)

Well, my neck was hurting so badly, I had to turn my whole body.

"I'll see you in therapy at 8:30 in the morning," he said.

There was no arguing with Dr. Le. I knew he had me, he knew he had me and all my faking that I was fine was done in vain.

Hearty Potato Salad

5 medium potatoes

4 hard boiled eggs

1/2 c. chopped dill pickles

1/4 c. chopped celery

2/3 c. salad dressing

2 T. mustard

2 T. vinegar

salt and pepper to taste

Mash hot potatoes slightly. Lightly mix everything else in and serve. Keep cold for tailgating.

Cheese Balls

1 c. pecans, chopped

1 lb. blue cheese

2 lbs. cream cheese

1 sm. pkg. processed sharp cheddar, grated

1 onion, finely minced

1 tsp. Worcestershire sauce

salt to taste

Set aside half the chopped pecans. Add the rest of them to the other ingredients. Blend well. Divide the mixture and shape into three balls. Roll in the remaining pecans and chill. Serve with crackers. These cheese balls can be made ahead of time and frozen.

Chris Mitchell
Oxford, Mississippi

The Chucky Mullins Courage Award

Chucky Mullins
July 8, 1969-May 6, 1991

The Chucky Mullins Courage Award, established in 1990 by Phi Beta Sigma fraternity, honors an outstanding defensive player each spring. The recipient has the honor of wearing Chucky's number, 38, the next season. The following players have won the award.

Chris Mitchell 1990	Alundis Brice 1994
Jeff Carter 1991	Michael Lowery 1995
Trea Southerland 1992	Derek Jones 1996
Johnny Dixon 1993	Nate Wayne 1997

George Barney Poole

Position & Years
End, 1941-42 & 1946-47

Nickname
Barney

All American (Army) 1944   College All-Star Game (c.) '49
All American (Army) 1946   SEC Skywriters All Time Team
All American (Ole Miss) 1947   Team of the Century
All American (Ole Miss) 1948   Miss. Sports Hall of Fame
All American Hon. Mention '43   Ole Miss Sports Hall of Fame

Momma's in the Stands

by Barney Poole

In 1947 I returned to play football at Ole Miss after a three-year stint at West Point as a member of the Army Cadet football squad. Although I enjoyed my time in the military, I couldn't wait to get back home to my family, friends, and Ole Miss football.

The 1947 season started off pretty good. John Vaught was our new head coach, and even though I had made All American at Army two years, I worked hard all summer to learn Coach Vaught's system. I wanted to earn a place on the team, and I didn't want people to say I didn't deserve my starting position.

Toward the end of the season, we were playing Chattanooga in Oxford. The game was pretty much a romp by us–something like 30-0 at the half. When we got to the dressing room, Coach Vaught told the first stringers to take off our uniforms because he wasn't going to let us play anymore.

As we started to undress, word came down from Billy Gates in the press box that Charlie Conerly had broken five or six college records in passing and I was within striking distance of the receiving record. Heck, I didn't even know what the receiving record was, but the coaches decided to put me back in the game.

And what did I do? I sat on the bench the whole third and about half of the fourth quarter. Then Coach Vaught put me back in the game to try to set the record.

We started running the little shuttle pass we used to pull behind the line of scrimmage. I'd catch the ball, run off tackle and then out of bounds to stop the clock. At this point all I was trying to do was catch some numbers. In fact, in the final ten plays, I caught eight passes and batted one down because it was in danger of being intercepted.

I wound up with something like 13 pass receptions, one short of the national receiving record.

On the last play of the game, right before the horn went off, I had caught another pass and got out of bounds. Well, a Chattanooga cornerback, who had had enough of us, got a 50-yard running start, charged me head-on as hard as he could and stuck me in the ribs with his shoulder pads or helmet or something.

Boy, did he ever knock the wind out of me! There I was lying on the ground, gasping for air and unable to move. My brother, Buster, the end coach, saw me and came over. He didn't kick me, but he did nudge me with his toe.

"Get up! That don't look good. Besides, Momma Poole is in the stands, and you're going to scare her to death," he scolded.

I wasn't hurt, but I wasn't getting any oxygen either. It didn't matter. I got up, trotted to the dressing room and saved my Momma a few more gray hairs.

Barney Poole played football for three teams during his collegiate career. His freshman and sophomore years, 1941 and 42, were spent at Ole Miss, where he played varsity ball both years. He then joined the Marines and was sent to B-12 School at the University of North Carolina where he became a member of their football team in 1943. This was his first time to be named as an Honorable Mention All American.

In 1944, Poole was appointed to the United States Military Academy and joined the Army team at West Point. During his tenure at the Academy, Army won the National Championship two consecutive years, and Poole was named All American in both 1944 and 1946.

Itching to get back to Mississippi and with no plans for a military career, he resigned his appointment from West Point in 1946. He returned to Ole Miss in 1947, where he played two more years, and was named All American again in 1947 and 1948. After attending three schools in eight years, Poole says he had enough hours for at least two degrees.

Five-hour Stew

6 carrots, sliced
5 celery stalks, chopped
3 potatoes, chopped bite size
1 large onion, finely chopped
2 lbs. stewing beef, cut in 1 inch chunks
2½ c. stewed tomatoes
1 box frozen lima beans
4 tsp. tapioca flour
salt and pepper to taste

Preheat oven to 250 degrees. Put everything in a large pot and bake for five hours.

Cheese Straws

1 lb. sharp cheddar cheese   *2 c. all-purpose flour*
1 to 2 sticks butter   *½ tsp. red pepper*

Preheat oven to 350 degrees. Grate cheese. Cut butter over it, and warm until soft enough to cream. Sift salt, peppers, and flour over the cheese and butter mixture. Add and mix (like biscuit dough). Use cookie press with star attachment and place on cookie sheet. Bake for 20 minutes or until done. Keeps well for a couple of weeks. Store in airtight containers.

Barney Poole
Gloster, Mississippi

143

Ray Poole

Position & Years
End, 1941-42 & 46

All SEC 1946   Miss. Sports Hall of Fame
Team Captain 1946   Ole Miss Sports Hall of Fame
Distinguished American Award

Reminiscing

by Ray Poole

Editor's Note: When you've been involved with Ole Miss football as long as Ray Poole has, there is no way you can tell just one story. Here are several short tales that Coach Poole shared with me. I just had to share all of them with you.

Bombs Bursting Everywhere

In 1941, right before World War II, Ole Miss was picked to win the SEC. Unfortunately, Mississippi State beat us and we didn't get to go to the Orange Bowl. A week after our devastating defeat, Pearl Harbor was bombed. It was hard to tell at that time which was harder to take, our defeat by State or the defeat of Pearl Harbor by the Japanese.

Going Bowling

When I think of my time at Ole Miss, I like to remember my coaching days. My memories of coaching the Rebels are vivid. During the first 19 years I coached, we went to 18 bowl games, so we had a pretty good record.

Recruiting

Part of my duties as a coach included recruiting. Before we decided to recruit tailback Doug Cunningham, I had to go watch him three times to make sure his legs were strong enough to carry him. Not only could they carry him, they took him all the way to the pros. He was one good football player.

Vaught Returns

In 1973, Coach John Vaught came out of retirement in mid-season to lead the Rebels. He never believed in running out with the team; he'd just walk behind them. So there all we coaches were, walking out with him at his first game back as head coach. We were playing the University of Southern Mississippi.

About the third play of the game, Southern ran an end sweep, and the back ran right into our bench. The first person he hit was Coach Vaught. Well, instead of catching himself to keep from falling down he grabbed his hair piece with both hands and fell over backwards. We sure had fun watching the films of that the next day.

The Players

I remember many Ole Miss teammates, classmates, players and friends I made and still have. Most of them have turned out to be outstanding citizens: doctors, lawyers, farmers, teachers and coaches.

You can't imagine how much it helped us during recruiting to have so many Ole Miss graduates in towns and cities across Mississippi and the south. They would talk to kids about Ole Miss, share their stories and help us convince the players we wanted that Ole Miss was the place for them to be.

Poole Drive

A couple of years ago, the University honored our family by naming a street after us. Being one of the oldest of the Poole group there, I was asked to say a few words. I thanked the University and the people who had come to the ceremony.

I thanked the press. I told them I appreciated their not saying anything negative about our family, and how the press had always given my brothers, cousins and me such positive coverage.

After I got home, I started thinking about what I had said, and then thought I probably had spoken a little bit out of turn. I remembered one time when the media didn't compliment me.

When I was a sophomore, Ole Miss had been picked to be Number One in the nation. A reporter from a leading publication came down to see us practice. When practice was over, Coach Harry Mehre called us over to meet the reporter. It was then he told us he was picking us number one.

That summer I was working construction in Birmingham, Alabama, and a guy from another school came over and told me about a good article on Ole Miss in a popular sports magazine.

I went to get the issue. The article was great. It had pictures of the star players, returning lettermen, stats, stories, and the player roster. It finally named all the freshmen. I got down to the last line, which read, "And don't forget, they have Ray Poole, who is greener than grass."

I just didn't think that was very complimentary.

Quick Chocolate Fudge

3 c. sugar   ¾ c. evaporated milk
½ c. cocoa   1½ sticks margarine
3 T. light corn syrup   1 c. pecans

Stir all together in a large pot. Bring to a rolling boil that you cannot stir down. Boil hard 2 1/2 minutes. Cool slightly and add a cup of pecans. Beat until it starts to get hard. Pour on a platter, cut or break when it gets hard. This is delicious.

Ray Poole
Oxford, Mississippi

Crab Spread

1 lb. crabmeat   1 tsp. lemon juice
¾ c. mayonnaise   2 T. parsley, chopped
1 tsp. Worcestershire sauce

Mix all ingredients. Chill at least four hours. Serve with your favorite crackers.

One night the Ole Miss basketball court was totally under water. Not literally, but five Pooles were on the court. Ray, Oliver, Flemin, Phillip and Barney, cousins and brothers, started one game.

Richard Price

Position & Years
Left Guard 1958-60

Nickname
Possum

All SEC 1959 & 60
Sophomore All SEC 1958
Senior Bowl 1961

Distinguished American Award
Ole Miss Sports Hall of Fame

Major Dad

by Richard Price

When I left for Ole Miss after my senior year in Vicksburg, I had one thing on my mind–playing football.

I left high school with many honors, among them, Scholastic All American. A small boy from a little town, I went straight to the School of Engineering and signed up. Yep, when I grew up, I'd be an engineer. Sounded good to me.

When I got to Ole Miss, I just kind of went crazy. I had never seen so many beautiful girls. Everywhere I looked, there stood another gorgeous Ole Miss coed. And parties, man, there was always a party going on somewhere, and I don't think I missed one of them. To tell you the truth, I did some pretty bad things my freshman year. I was your proverbial hell raiser.

At the end of the semester, I passed only one hour, and that was football. Not much to be proud of, that's for sure.

Well, before I knew it, Coach Vaught called me to his office. Now you've never met such a gentleman. He was so proper and always had a way of making us feel at ease.

He said in his most familiar voice, "Sonny, we're going to have to change your major."

Which they did, to education. I had to have 30 hours to play my sophomore year. I got them next semester and in summer school. I did, indeed, play the rest of my sophomore year, followed by two more of the most fun and exciting years of my life.

What Coach Vaught said:

Richard was smart enough to do his college work; it was just a matter of putting him in the right major. He had to pass because you don't get many talents like him. He was so talented.

He's a fine, outstanding gentleman. I'm happy that I was in football when I see prospects turn out like Richard did and watch the change he made in his life from the time he got here until he graduated. It just makes me happy I had something to do with it.

Italian Cream Cheese Cake

2 c. sugar
2 sticks margarine
5 eggs
1 c. buttermilk

2 c. flour
1 tsp. baking soda
1 tsp. vanilla
1 c. coconut

Preheat oven to 350 degrees. Cream sugar and butter. Stir in eggs, one at a time. Add buttermilk, flour, soda, vanilla, and coconut. Blend well. Bake 18 to 20 minutes in a 9x12 pan. Cool in pan for 5 minutes, remove from pan to wire rack and cool thoroughly. After cooling, cut cake in half and then cut each half horizontally to make 4 layers.

Frosting

1 8 oz. pkg. cream cheese
¾ stick margarine
1 box powdered sugar

1 tsp. vanilla
2 c. pecans, chopped

Mix all ingredients thoroughly, then add pecans.

This cake is better with a double batch of frosting.

Rebel Mary

1 T. celery salt
1 T. salt
1 5 oz. bottle Worcestershire sauce
8-10 drops hot sauce
½ c. lemon juice
hot and spicy vegetable juice

Mix all ingredients in a gallon jar. Fill to the top with vegetable juice. Shake well and refrigerate. Serve ice cold.

Richard Price
Columbia, Mississippi

TAILGATING SUGGESTIONS
FOR THE GROVE

The Grove opens at 7 a.m. on game days.

Only University events may be held in a reserved place. All other spaces are on first-come basis.

Only occupy the amount of space you need.

Avoid using ropes, ribbons or stakes to reserve an area.

Avoid driving stakes into the ground. The Grove has underground electric and water lines.

No solicitation is allowed.

If you bring a large grill, set it up on the perimeter of the Grove. This keeps little Rebels who are playing ball safe.

Clean up before you leave.

Be courteous. After all, we are family.

Please follow these guidelines when tailgating in the Grove.

Do You Know
These Ole Miss Facts?

Ole Miss has:

Three national titles in the NCAA Record Book
    1959 Dunkle System
    1960 Football Writers, Dunkle System, Williamson System
    1962 Litkenhous Ratings

Six SEC Championships
    1947, 54, 55, 60, 62 & 63

Participated in 25 bowl games, 15 consecutively

Won 14 bowl games

15 bowl MVP's

35 first-team All Americans

15 Academic All Americans

7 National Football Foundation Scholarship Winners

More than 150 professional players

The SEC Team of the Decade (1950-59)

16 NCAA individual champions

10 NCAA team statistical champions

Todd Sandroni

Position & Years
Free Safety 1987-90

All SEC 1987 & 88
Academic All American 1989
Academic All American 1990
Academic All SEC 1987-90
Toyota Leadership Award 1990

National Asso. of Collegiate
  Athletic Directors/Disney
  Scholar-Athlete Award 1991
Team of the Century

Hama to Bama

by Todd Sandroni

On October 8, 1988, Coach Billy Brewer's birthday, we gave him a gift no Ole Miss coach had gotten in 24 years.

We were 17-point underdogs against Alabama. It was their homecoming game. The Tide was rolling. Earlier in the day the University had dedicated the Bear Bryant Museum. Victory was in the air and they smelled it. It was a smell they had come to know. Their fans outnumbered ours by thousands, or so it seemed.

The day of the game Coach Brewer showed us the local newspaper. Their sportswriters had predicted we'd lose by 35 points. We weren't feeling especially happy about that prediction, and besides, we took that a little bit personally. After all, who were they to have us defeated before the game even started?

We scored 15 points in the final 46 seconds of that game to upset the 12th ranked Crimson Tide 22-12. And to put the icing on *his* cake, our secondary held them to zero pass completions with three interceptions.

As Coach James "T" Thomas said, "We put the hama to Bama!"

I still wonder what their fans thought after the game, and I bet those guys who played that day still relive the agony of defeat by a team they were supposed to beat by 35 points.

Shrimp Dip

1 can broken shrimp
1 8 oz. pkg. cream cheese
1 8 oz. carton sour cream

¼ c. mayonnaise
1 pkg. dry Italian dressing mix
1 tsp. lemon juice

Drain can of shrimp. Pour lemon juice over the shrimp. Let set while mixing the remaining ingredients. Pour shrimp into mixture and stir. This is better if made a day ahead of time. Best served with corn chips.

Todd Sandroni
Tupelo, Mississippi

Nutty Muffins

3 eggs, beaten lightly
1 c. brown sugar
½ c. flour
¼ tsp. baking powder

¼ tsp. salt
1 c. pecans, chopped
vanilla to taste

Preheat oven to 325 degrees. Mix all ingredients. Bake in small muffin tins until lightly browned.

Cheesy Crackers

1½ c. flour
1 stick oleo
½ sharp cheddar, grated

½ tsp. red pepper
dash salt
1 c. pecans, finely chopped

Blend ingredients with mixer. Shape into rolls about the size of a silver dollar. Wrap in waxed paper or plastic wrap. Refrigerate. When firm, slice into 1/4 inch wafers. Bake at 450 degrees for 10 to 12 minutes. Store in airtight container.

In 1985, Head Coach Billy Brewer began the tradition of having the Ole Miss Football Team walk through the Grove on their way to Vaught-Hemingway Stadium.

Astroturf was laid in Hemingway Stadium in 1971, making it the only stadium in the state with an artificial surface. The turf was removed from the field in 1988 and replaced with prescription athletic turf.

Marvin Terrell

Position & Years
Guard 1957-59

Nicknames
Boy & T.V.

All American 1959
All SEC 1959
Atlanta Constitution
  Superlatives, SEC Lineman
  of the Year 1959

Birmingham Quarterback Club
  Most Valuable Lineman 1959
SEC Outstanding Lineman '59
Team of the Century
Ole Miss Sports Hall of Fame

The Naked Truth

by Marvin Terrell

During my playing days at Ole Miss, we would have M Club initiation once a year. As athletes would letter in their respective sports, we would have a night set aside for initiation.

Everybody would go to the field house and then we would do various things to the initiates. Some were pretty bad, but most were done in fun. At the end of the night, all the initiates were stripped to their "birthday suits" and had to make it back to the dorm across campus as best they could.

Ralph "Catfish" Smith thought all the hiding and running from tree to tree was silly so he just took off running across campus, in the raw. He ran past the library just as it was closing. He then darted into the "grill" where the post office was. There he decided to stop and check his mailbox. That done, he ran right out the front door and down the street to Miller Hall. He told us that a lot of students had seen him and done double takes. Believe it or not, he didn't quite understand why.

The Michael S. Starnes Athletic Training Center was made possible by a donation of $1 million toward the facility by Michael Starnes of Memphis. A 1968 graduate of Ole Miss, he is the chairman and chief executive officer of M.S. Carriers, Inc.

The facility, formally Doc Knight Field House, includes a state–of–the–art training room, 13 treatment tables, a wet room with whirlpool, a massive weight room, and various conference rooms and offices.

Dr. Jerry Hollingsworth, an Ole Miss alumnus, joined with Archie Manning to establish a recruitment/memorabilia center in the facility. Hollingsworth/Manning Hall provides a place for coaches to meet recruits and showcases Ole Miss sports trophies.

Hollingsworth, a Fort Walton, Florida, physician, made a $2 million contribution to the University. Part of his gift went to setting up Hollingsworth/Manning Hall.

Ragin' Rebel Red Beans & Rice with Sausage

1 pkg. red beans	salt and pepper
garlic salt	bay leaves to taste
seasoned salt	onions
Worcestershire sauce	smoked sausage

Soak a package of red beans overnight in water. Drain, add fresh water and slow cook in an iron pot. Add your favorite seasonings, plus cut-up onions, and my favorite, bay leaves. Cook slowly for several hours. Add smoked sausage for the last hour of cooking. Serve hot over cooked or steamed rice.

Marvin Terrell
Yazoo City, Mississippi

Banana Nut Cake

$2^{1}/_{4}$ c. sifted cake flour
2 tsp. double-acting baking powder
$^{1}/_{2}$ tsp. soda
1 tsp. salt
$1^{1}/_{2}$ c. sugar
1 c. ripe banana, mashed
1 tsp. lemon juice
$^{2}/_{3}$ c. buttermilk
$^{1}/_{2}$ c. shortening
2 eggs
1 tsp. vanilla
$^{1}/_{2}$ c. nuts, chopped

Preheat oven to 350 degrees. Sift first five ingredients together. Combine with banana and lemon juice. Add buttermilk and shortening. Beat for two minutes, blend on low and then beat on medium until batter is well mixed. Add eggs and vanilla. Beat for two more minutes. Fold in nuts. Pour into a well greased and lightly floured pan. Bake 30 to 35 minutes.

Wesley Walls

Position & Years
Tightend 1985-88

All American 1988
All SEC 1988
Academic All SEC 1986-88
All-SEC Team of the 1980's
Team Co-Captain 1988

Clower-Walters Scholarship
NCAA Postgraduate
 Scholarship 1989
Jackson Touchdown Club
 Sportsman of the Year 1989

Winning with the Draw

by Wesley Walls

My senior year, 1988, we were playing Alabama at their homecoming, which was also the day they were dedicating the stadium to the late, great, Paul "Bear" Bryant.

It was a defensive battle all day. In fact, it was 0-0 at the end of the first half. We kicked off to start the second half and they ran the ball back for a touchdown, the first score of the game. But, the great part of this battle was just beginning.

Earlier in the game, Shawn Sykes, an outstanding running back from West Point, had injured his knee. Thankfully he was able to come back in, because we needed him badly in the second half. We called a draw play, gave him the ball and he hobbled almost 60 yards, dragging defenders, for a touchdown.

We still needed a score to win, and we wanted that win bad. So what did we do? We ran the same draw play again and there goes Shawn, right into the end zone, never touched.

A great hush came over the stadium. Some said the only noise heard was the sound of the great Bear Bryant rolling over in his grave.

From 1848 until 1871, The University of Mississippi was the only state institution of higher learning in Mississippi. And for 110 years, it was the only institution in the state consistently designated as a university.

The first class graduated in 1851. In 1854 the School of Law, the nation's fourth oldest state supported law school, was authorized by the state Legislature.

In 1882, women were admitted, and in 1885, Sarah McGehee Isom, became a member of the faculty, making The University of Mississippi one of the first in the South to hire a woman faculty member.

Fried Chicken
with
White Milk Gravy

Fried Chicken

4 to 6 boneless, skinless chicken breasts
enough flour to coat chicken well
red pepper to taste
garlic salt to taste
oil for frying

Sprinkle red pepper and garlic salt directly on chicken. Add red pepper and garlic salt to flour. Coat chicken with flour mix. Put enough oil in a frying pan to cover the bottom completely. Fry over medium heat until golden brown, turning each side only once.

White Milk Gravy

2 c. milk   *1 tsp. oil*
2 T. flour   *salt and pepper*

Mix together milk and flour. Put 1 teaspoon of oil in a pan over medium heat. Pour in milk and flour mixture until it thickens. Salt and pepper to taste.

Great with canned or homemade biscuits.

Wesley Walls
Charlotte, North Carolina

Citronella candles come in handy after the game. Take them for light and to keep the bugs away.

Ben Williams

Position & Years
Defensive Tackle 1972-75

Nickname
Gentle Ben

All American 1975
All SEC 1973, 74 & 75
SEC All Rookie Team 1972
East West Bowl 1975
Senior Bowl 1976

All America Bowl 1976
Colonel Rebel
Team of the Century
Miss. Sports Hall of Fame
Ole Miss Sports Hall of Fame

Into the Arena

by Ben Williams

I was the first black athlete at Ole Miss. Many people have asked me what that was like. Here's the answer.

In my sophomore year of high school in Yazoo City, Yazoo City High School won the Big 8 Championship. Because the schools were not integrated at that time, I attended an all-black high school across town. The following year, however, we did integrate and I transferred to Yazoo High. That's how Coach Junie Hovious of Ole Miss found me.

Outstanding senior Larry Kramer was a hot recruit and Coach Hovious really came down to scout him. I was just a junior, but I guess I caught Hovious' eye because he started recruiting me too. By my senior year, other colleges were interested in me: Jackson State, Alcorn, Mississippi State, and Southern, but Coach Hovious was persistent.

Keep in mind, I'm just a country boy from Yazoo City, but the thought of going to Ole Miss to play football really appealed to me. When I went up for a visit, I just fell in love with it. Everyone was so nice to me, and I thought the University was beautiful. Coach Hovious talked to my grandmother about my signing a scholarship and she and I thought it was a good idea.

So I signed with Ole Miss, not really even realizing I was the first black athlete there. I was lucky because my freshman year, the SEC had changed its rule to allow freshmen to play varsity ball. I got to play, which I thought was a very big honor for a freshman. I loved every minute of it.

People ask me quite often if I was scared about going to Ole Miss as the first black athlete, but I tell them no, I wasn't scared. And do you know why? Because football is different from most other things in life. When you play, it's almost like you're in an arena. You have to compete. When you get in the arena, race is not a problem; it just doesn't make any difference. In fact, playing football at Ole Miss was the most pleasant experience I've ever had.

Chicken Salad

3 c. cold, cooked, skinless chicken breasts
1 c. celery, diced
½ c. green onions, chopped
½ c. sweet green pepper, minced
2 c. Granny Smith apples, chopped
4 boiled eggs, chopped
salt and pepper to taste
MSG and lemon pepper to taste
mayonnaise to moisten
1 T. sugar
1 tsp. parsley, minced

Mix all ingredients except parsley. Cover and chill 2 to 3 hours. Garnish with parsley and serve.

Gentle Ben's Baked Beans

2 16 oz. cans pork and beans
½ c. onions, chopped
1 c. bell pepper, chopped
¼ c. brown sugar

1 tsp. mustard
1 lb. ground beef
¼ c. barbecue sauce

Preheat oven to 350 degrees. Brown ground beef, onions and bell pepper. Pour off grease. Place pork and beans in casserole dish. Add ground beef mixture, brown sugar, mustard and barbecue sauce. Bake until bubbly.

Ben Williams
Jackson, Mississippi

OleMiss

Ben Williams played under three different head coaches at Ole Miss; Billy Kinard (1972), John Vaught (1973) and Ken Cooper (1974).

RECIPE LISTING

A

Adams, Billy Ray   16

Present Hometown
  Madison, MS
Wife
  Dorothy
Children
  Brad
  David
Nickname
  Tiger
Position
  Fullback
Years played at Ole Miss 1959-61
All American 1961
All SEC 1961
Team of the Decade, 1959
Miss. Sports Hall of Fame
Ole Miss Sports Hall of Fame

Alford, Warner   20

Present Hometown
  Ridgeland, MS
Wife
  Kay
Children
  Swayze
  Phyllis
  John
Nickname
  Boon
Position
  Left Guard
Years played at Ole Miss 1958-60
Team Co-Captain 1960
Distinguished American Award
Team of the Decade 1959

B

Brewer, Billy   24

Present Hometown
  Oxford, MS
Wife
  Kay
Children
  Brett
  Gunter
Nickname
  Dog

Position
  Quarterback, Defensive Back
Years played at Ole Miss 1957-59
All SEC 1959
College All-Star Game 1960
Team of the Century
Professional
Washington Redskins 1960-62

Brewer, Johnny   28

Present Hometown
  Vicksburg, MS
Wife
  Anita
Children
  Jonnita Barrett
  John, Jr.
  Bradley Sean
Nicknames
  Stud, Tonto, Jungle, Leg & Cheyenne
Position
  End
Years played at Ole Miss 1957 & 59-60
All American 1959 & 60
All SEC 1959 & 60
MVP SEC Offensive lineman 1959 & 60
Senior Bowl 1961
All America Bowl Game 1961
College All-Star Game 1961
Ole Miss Sports Hall of Fame
Professional
Cleveland Browns 1961-67
New Orleans Saints 1968-70
All Pro Rookie Team 1961
Cleveland Touchdown Club
  MVP Defensive Player 1966

Brown, Allen   32

Present Hometown
  Ferriday, LA
Wife
  Margaret
Children
  Tim
  Jodi
  Burkes
Nickname
  Red
Position
  Tight End
Years played at Ole Miss 1962-64

Brown, Allen (contd.)

All American 1964
All SEC 1963 & 64
Sophomore All SEC 1962
Team Co-Captain 1964
Blue-Gray Game 1964
Senior Bowl 1965
College All-Star Game 1965
Ole Miss Sports Hall of Fame
Professional
Green Bay Packers (3 Years)
NFL Championship Team 1965
Played in Super Bowls I & II 1967 & 68

C

Conerly, Charlie (deceased) 37

Wife
   Perian
Nickname
   Chunkin' Charlie & Roach
Position
   Tailback
Years played at Ole Miss 1942 & 46-47
Consensus All American 1947
All Time SEC Team
All SEC 1946 & 47
4th in Heisman voting 1947
Ole Miss Hall of Fame
Team Captain 1947
SEC Skywriters All-Time SEC Team
Atlanta Touchdown Club SEC Back of the
   Year 1947
Nashville Banner SEC Player of the Year
   1947
College All-Star Game 1948
Athlon Sports All Time Rebel Team
Distinguished American Award
Helms Athletic Hall of Fame
National Football Hall of Fame
Team of Century
Miss. Sports Hall of Fame
Ole Miss Sports Hall of Fame
Professional
New York Giants (14 years)
Rookie of the Year 1948
NFL Most Valuable Player 1959
All-Professional 1948 & 57-59
Led Giants to World Championship in
   1956 and to four division titles.

Crespino, Bobby   40

Present Hometown
   Macon, MS
Wife
   Barbara
Children
   Lou Mitchener
   Robert
   Joe
Nickname
   Pluto
Position
   Right Halfback
Years played at Ole Miss 1958-60
All Star Game, Outstanding South Team
   Back 1961
Senior Bowl 1961
All America Bowl 1961
Miss. Sports Hall of Fame
Ole Miss Sports Hall of Fame
Professional
1st. Round Draft Pick Cleveland Browns
   1961
Cleveland Browns 1961-63
New York 1964-68

Cunningham, Doug   45

Present Hometown
   Jackson, MS
Nickname
   Legs
Position
   Tailback
Years played at Ole Miss 1964-66
All SEC 1966
Team Co-Captain
Colonel Rebel
Ole Miss Sports Hall of Fame
Professional
San Francisco 49er's 1967-73
Washington Redskins 1974

D

Day, Eagle   48

Present Hometown
   Jackson, MS
Wife
   Jo Anne
Children
   Diana

167

Elmore, Doug (contd.)
Professional
Washington Redskins 1962
Calgary 1963

F

Farragut, Ken   64
Present Hometown
   Flourtown, PA
Wife
   Jane
Children
   Deborah J. Worstall
   Kenneth
   J. Daniel
Nickname
   Dynamite
Position
   Center
Years played at Ole Miss 1947-50
All American Honorable Mention
Team Captain 1950
College All-Star Game
Ole Miss Sports Hall of Fame
Professional
Philadelphia Eagles 1951-54
Pro Bowl 1954

Fitzsimmons, Mike   68
Present Hometown
   Eads, TN
Wife
   Kimberly Ann
Children
   Erin
   Michael
Nickname
   Fitz
Position
   Defensive Tackle
Years played at Ole Miss 1983-86
All American Honorable Mention 1986
All SEC 1986
Team Co-Captain 1986
SEC Player of the Week
Hinds County Chapter Most Dedicated
   Player Award 1987
Memphis Player of the Year 1987

Flowers, Charlie   72
Present Hometown
   Atlanta, GA
Wife
   Sharon
Children
   Julie
   Charlie, Jr.
   Ashley
Nickname
   Big Car
Position
   Fullback
Years played at Ole Miss 1957-59
All American 1959
All SEC 1958 & 59
All South 1959
Academic All American 1959
Academic All SEC 1958 & 59
Team Co-Captain 1959
Athlon Sports All-Time Rebel Team
All Time Bowl Teams, Sugar
Distinguished American Award
Team of the Century
Miss. Sports Hall of Fame
Ole Miss Sports Hall of Fame
Professional
San Diego (AFL) 1960-61
New York (AFL) 1962

Fourcade, John   76
Present Hometown
   Harvey, LA
Nickname
   Mississippi Gambler
Position
   Quarterback
Years played at Ole Miss 1978-81
All SEC 1979 & 80
Team Co-Captain 1981
Sophomore All SEC 1979
Sophomore of the Year 1979
Senior Bowl MVP Offense 1981
Who's Who 1981
Ole Miss Hall of Fame 1981
Colonel Rebel
John Vaught Award of Excellence 1982
Professional
British Columbia (CFL) 1982
Memphis (USFL) 1984
New Orleans Saints 1987-90

169

Franklin, Bobby   80

Present Hometown
   Senatobia, MS
Wife
   JoAn
Children
   Ray
   Ashley
Nicknames
   Waxie & One Shot
Position
   Quarterback
Years played at Ole Miss 1957-59
All SEC 1958
MVP Gator Bowl 1958
MVP Cotton Bowl 1958
MVP Sugar Bowl 1960
All Time Bowl Team-Sugar 1960
College All-Star Game 1960
Distinguished American Award
Ole Miss Sports Hall of Fame
Professional
Cleveland Browns (7 years)

G

Gibbs, Jake   85

Present Hometown
   Oxford, MS
Wife
   Tricia
Children
   Dean
   Monte
   Frank
Nickname
   Jake
Position
   Quarterback
Years played at Ole Miss 1958-60
All American 1960
All SEC 1959 & 60
Team Co-Captain 1960
MVP Sugar Bowl 1961
Best Back in SEC 1960
3rd in Heisman Votes 1960
National Football Hall of Fame
Miss. Sports Hall of Fame
Ole Miss Sports Hall of Fame
Baseball

All American 1960 & 61
All SEC 1959, 60 & 61
All District III 1960 & 61
Professional Baseball
N.Y. Yankees (10 years)

Grantham, Larry   88

Present Hometown
   Horn Lake, MS
Wife
   Peggy
Children
   LeAnne
   James Larry, II
Position
   End
Years played at Ole Miss 1957-59
All SEC Sophomore Team
All SEC 1958 & 59
Team of the Century
Miss. Sports Hall of Fame
Ole Miss Sports Hall of Fame
Professional
New York Jets (13 years)
All AFL (6 years)
Seven All Star games

Griffing, Glynn   92

Present Hometown
   Jackson, MS
Wife
   Monica (Nikki)
Children
   Kim
   Sandi
Position
   Quarterback
Years play at Ole Miss 1960-62
All American 1962
All SEC 1962
Team Co-Captain 1962
Atlanta Touchdown Club Award, SEC
   Back of the Year
Sugar Bowl, Outstanding Player, 1963
Senior Bowl, Outstanding Player, 1963
College All-Star Game 1963
Coaches Asso. All America Bowl 1963
Ole Miss Sports Hall of Fame
Professional
New York Giants (NFL) 1963

H

Hall, Parker   96

Present Hometown
  Vicksburg, MS
Wife
  Josephine (deceased)
Children
  Parker
  Tully
  Chris
  Peter
Nickname
  Bullet
Position
  Halfback
Years played at Ole Miss 1936-38
All American 1938
All SEC 1938
All-South 1938
SEC Scoring Champion 1938
College All-Star Game 1939
Distinguished American Award
National Football Hall of Fame
Miss. Sports Hall of Fame
Ole Miss Sports Hall of Fame
Professional
Cleveland NFL 1939-41
San Francisco All American Conf. 1946
All Pro 1939
NFL Rookie of the Year 1939
NFL Player of the Year 1939

Harrison, Harry   100

Present Hometown
  Brandon, MS
Children
  Nick
  Josh
Nickname
  Horse
Position
  Safety
Years played at Ole Miss 1971-73
All American 1973
All SEC 1973
Academic All SEC 1972
SEC Interception Champion 1972
Ole Miss Sports Hall of Fame

Hindman, Stan   104

Present Hometown
  Oakland, CA
Wife
  Anna Scott
Children
  Kate
  Silas
Nickname
  Haystack
Position
  Right Guard
Years played at Ole Miss 1963-65
All American 1965
All SEC 1963, 64 & 65
Team Co-Captain 1965
Sophomore All SEC
Academic All American 1965
Academic All SEC 1965
Birmingham Quarterback Club Quarter
  Century All SEC Team 1950-75
College All-Star Game 1966
Senior Bowl, Mobile, 1966
Coaches Asso. All America Bowl 1965
SEC Skywriters All Time SEC Team
Athlon Sports All Time Rebel Team
Team of the Century
Miss. Sports Hall of Fame
Ole Miss Sports Hall of Fame
Professional
San Francisco, 1966-71 & 1973-74

Hovious, Junie   108

Present Hometown
  Oxford, MS
Wife
  Kitty (deceased)
  Anne (deceased)
Children
  John William
  Bradford Weldon
  Allen Lee
  Robert Lawrence
Nickname
  Junie
Position
  Left Halfback
Years played at Ole Miss 1939-41
All SEC 1939, 40 & 41

171

Hovious, Junie (contd.)

All Decade (1933-42) Team
Blue/Gray Game MVP 1941
Invited to College All Star Game 1942
Sport Letterman
Colonel Rebel
Distinguished American Award
Miss. Sports Hall of Fame
Ole Miss Hall of Fame
Professional
New York Giants (1 year) 1945

K

Khayat, Robert 112

Present Hometown
  Oxford, MS
Wife
  Margaret
Children
  Margaret K. Bratt
  Robert, Jr.
Position
  Place Kicker
Years played at Ole Miss 1957-59
College All-Star Game 1960
Academic All American
Distinguished American Award
Team of the Century
Ole Miss Sports Hall of Fame
Baseball
All SEC Baseball
Professional
Washington Redskins 1960-63
Pro Bowl 1961

L

Lear, Jimmy 116

Present Hometown
  Indianola, MS
Wife
  Joanne
Children
  Annette L.Watson
  Elizabeth L. McCarty
  James, III
Nickname
  "King" Lear
Position
  Quarterback

Years played at Ole Miss 1950-52
All American 1952
All SEC 1951 & 52
Colonel Rebel
Ole Miss Hall of Fame
Miss. Sports Hall of Fame
Ole Miss Sports Hall of Fame

Lee, Brian 121

Present Hometown
  Atlanta, GA
Position
  Kicker
Years played at Ole Miss 1989-92
Academic All American, Dist. 6
Academic All SEC
SEC Player of the Week 1991
All-Time Leading Scorer
Most Field Goals in One Game

M

Mangum, Kris 124

Present Hometown
  Charlotte, NC
Position
  Tight end
Years played at Ole Miss 1994-96
All American 1996
All American Honorable Mention 1995
All SEC 1995 & 96
Professional
Drafted by Carolina Panthers 1996

Manning, Archie 128

Present Hometown
  New Orleans, LA
Wife
  Olivia
Children
  Cooper
  Peyton
  Eli
Position
  Quarterback
Years played at Ole Miss 1968-70
All American 1969 & 70
All Time All American
All SEC 1969 & 70
All South 1970
Team Co-Captain 1970

172

Manning, Archie (contd.)

Outstanding College Back in America
1969
Nashville Banner Award, SEC Player of
the Year, 1969
Coach and Athlete Award, Player of the
Year in Southeastern Area, 1969
UPI SEC, Offensive Player of the Year,
1969
Sportsman of the Year 1969
Atlanta Touchdown Club, SEC Back of
the Year, 1969
Birmingham Quarterback Club Quarter
Century All SEC Team 1969
SEC Outstanding Back 1969 & 1970
Sugar Bowl Outstanding Player 1970
Gator Bowl Award, Most Valuable Player,
Losing Team, 1971
Hula Bowl 1971
25 Year (1961-85) All SEC Team
SEC Skywriters All SEC Team (1933-82)
Lakeland Ledger 25 Year (1961-85) All
SEC Team
Byron "Whizzer" White Humanitarian
Award, 1978
Sports Illustrated National Back of the
Week 1969
AP National Back of the Week 1968 & 69
UPI Offensive Player of the Year 1969
All SEC Team 1960's and 70's
Athlon Sports All Time Rebel Team
Jackson Touchdown Club, Sportsman of
the Year, 1969
National Football Hall of Fame
Team of the Century
Miss. Sports Hall of Fame
Ole Miss Sports Hall of Fame
Professional
First round Draft Pick
New Orleans Saints (10 years)
All Pro 1978

Mims, Crawford   132

Present Hometown
Vicksburg, MS
Wife
Betty "Boop"
Children
Renee Mims Boyce
Crawford Jr.

John Howard Vaught
Paul David
Peter Lloyd
Position
Right Guard
Years played at Ole Miss 1951-53
Consensus All American 1953
AP All American
UP All American
Look All American
National Broadcasting Company All
American
Sportswriters Association All American
Coaches All American
Philip Morris All American
Tempo All America
All SEC 1952 & 53
All South 1953
Jacobs Blocking Award 1953
MVP North South Shrine Bowl 1953
All Star Game 1954
Athlon Sports All Time Rebel Team
Mississippi Sports Hall of Fame
Ole Miss Sports Hall of Fame

Mitchell, Chris   136

Present Hometown
Oxford, MS
Wife
Sharon Kay
Children
Christopher Alexander, II
Sidney Leigh-Anne
Nickname
Creek
Position
Safety
Years played at Ole Miss 1987-90
All American Honorable Mention 1990
All SEC 1990
Team Co-Captain 1990
Chucky Mullins Courage Award first
recipient
Sports Illustrated Player of the Week
Gillette Player of the Week
Senior Bowl 1991
Team of the Century
Professional
Philadelphia Eagles 1991
Orlando Thunder 1992

P

Poole, George Barney   140

Present Hometown
  Gloster, MS
Wife
  Martha
Children
  Janet
  Jodie
Nickname
  Barney
Position
  End
Years played at Ole Miss 1941-42, 46-47
All American Honorable Mention 1943
All American 1944 & 46 (Army)
All American 1947 & 48 (Ole Miss)
All SEC 1947 & 48
College All-Star Game 1949 (captain)
Appointed to West Point 1944
Ole Miss Hall of Fame
National Football Hall of Fame
Helms Athletic Foundation Hall of Fame
SEC Skywriter's All-Time SEC Team
Athlon Sports All Time Rebel Team
Team of the Century
Miss. Sports Hall of Fame
Ole Miss Sports Hall of Fame
Professional
New York Yankees (1 year) All American
  Conference
New York Yanks (2 years)
Dallas Texans (1 year)

Poole, Ray   144

Present Hometown
  Oxford, MS
Wife
  Wanda
Children
  Ray, Jr.
  Patti Sanders
Position
  End
Years played at Ole Miss 1941, 42 & 46
Look All American
All SEC 1946
Team Captain 1946
9 Athletic letters

3 football
3 basketball
3 baseball
Distinguished American Award
Miss. Sports Hall of Fame
Ole Miss Sports Hall of Fame
Professional
N.Y. Giants 1947-52
Montreal 1953-54
All Pro 1950

Price, Richard   148

Present Hometown
  Columbia, MS
Wife
  Leigh
Children
  Latta
  Paige
Nickname
  Possum
Position
  Left guard
Years played at Ole Miss 1958-60
All SEC 1959 & 60
Sophomore All SEC 1958
Senior Bowl 1961
Distinguished American Award
Ole Miss Sports Hall of Fame

S

Sandroni, Todd   152

Present Hometown
  Tupelo, MS
Wife
  Lisa
Years played at Ole Miss 1987-90
Position
  Free Safety
All SEC 1987 & 88
Academic All American 1989 & 90
Academic All SEC 1987-90
Toyota Leadership Award 1990
National Association of Collegiate
  Athletic Directors/Disney Scholar
  Athlete Award 1991
Athlon Sports All Time Rebel Team
Team of the Century

T

Terrell, Marvin 156

Present Hometown
Yazoo City, MS
Wife
Lettie
Children
Jana
Julie
Nicknames
Boy & T.V.
Years played at Ole Miss 1957-59
Position
Guard
All American 1959
All SEC 1959
SEC Outstanding Lineman 1959
Senior Bowl 1960
Birmingham Quarterback Club Most
Valuable Lineman 1959
Atlanta Constitution Superlatives Lineman
of the Year 1959
Athlon Sports All Time Rebel Team
Team of the Century
Ole Miss Sports Hall of Fame
Professional
Dallas Texans (AFL) 1960-62
Kansas City Chiefs 1963
Toronto Argonauts 1964
AFL All Star Game 1962

W

Walls, Wesley 159

Present Hometown
Charlotte, NC
Wife
Christy
Children
Alexandria
Colton
Years played at Ole Miss 1985-88
Position
Tight End
All American 1988
All SEC 1988
Academic All SEC 1986, 87 & 88
All SEC Team of the 1980's
Team Co-Captain 1988

Clower-Walters Scholarship 1989
NCAA Postgraduate Scholarship 1989
Jackson Touchdown Club
Sportsman of the Year 1989
Athlon Sports All Time Rebel Team
Professional
San Francisco 49er's 1989-93
New Orleans Saints 1994-95
Carolina Panthers 1996
All Pro 1996

Williams, Ben 162

Present Hometown
Jackson, MS
Wife
Linda
Children
Rodrick
Aisha
Jarrett
Nickname
Gentle Ben
Years played at Ole Miss 1972-75
Position
Defensive Tackle
All American 1975
All SEC 1973, 74 & 75
Team Co-Captain 1975
AP National Lineman of the Week 1973
Colonel Rebel
Senior Bowl 1976
All America Bowl 1976
East-West Bowl 1975
Athlon Sports All Time Rebel Team
Distinguished American Award
Team of the Century
Ole Miss Hall of Fame
Miss. Sports Hall of Fame
Ole Miss Sports Hall of Fame
Professional
Buffalo Bills 1976-85
Pro Bowl 1982
Member Buffalo Bills Silver Anniversary
All-Time Team

175

Tale-Gating with Rebel Greats©

P.O. Box 820262
Vicksburg, MS 39182

Please send _____ copies of **Tale-Gating with Rebel Greats** at $16.95 plus $3.50 shipping & handling per copy. Mississippi residents add $1.19 per copy for sales tax.

Name: _____

Street Address: _____

City: _____ State: _____ Zip: _____

Charge to: ☐ MasterCard   ☐ Visa

Account number _____ Expiration Date: _____

Make checks payable to, **Tale-Gating with Rebel Greats**. 5% of the total wholesale sales of Tale-Gating with Rebel Greats will be donated to The J.W. Davidson All American Scholarship-Ole Miss M Club Chapter.

Tale-Gating with Rebel Greats©

P.O. Box 820262
Vicksburg, MS 39182

Please send _____ copies of **Tale-Gating with Rebel Greats** at $16.95 plus $3.50 shipping & handling per copy. Mississippi residents add $1.19 per copy for sales tax.

Name: _____

Street Address: _____

City: _____ State: _____ Zip: _____

Charge to: ☐ MasterCard   ☐ Visa

Account number _____ Expiration Date: _____

Make checks payable to, **Tale-Gating with Rebel Greats**. 5% of the total wholesale sales of Tale-Gating with Rebel Greats will be donated to The J.W. Davidson All American Scholarship-Ole Miss M Club Chapter.